Motherfoclóir

DARACH Ó SÉAGHDHA is the author of the popular twitter account @theirishfor, whose followers include Dara Ó Briain, Ed Byrne, Marian Keyes, Gerry Adams, Amy Huberman, the Rubberbandits, Colm O'Regan and Gráinne Seoige. He lives in Swords, Co. Dublin and is married, with one daughter.

MOTHERFOCLÓIR

Dispatches from a not so dead language

Darach Ó Séaghdha

First published in the UK in 2017 by Head of Zeus, Ltd.

Copyright © Darach Ó Séaghdha, 2017

9 7 5 4 6 8

A catalogue record for this book is available from
the British Library.

ISBN (HB): 9781786691866
ISBN (E): 9781786691859

Designed and typeset by Lindsay Nash

Printed and bound in Great Britain
by CPI Group (UK) Ltd, Croydon CR0 4YY

Head of Zeus Ltd
First Floor East
5–8 Hardwick Street
London EC1R 4RG
WWW.HEADOFZEUS.COM

For Dad, who gave me my love of language,
and
for Lasairíona, to whom I will try to pass that on

'Don't you love the dictionary?
When I first read it, I thought it was a really,
really, long poem about everything.'

David Bowie

CONTENTS

CONTENTS

FOREWORD

This may come as a surprise to generations of Irish pupils, but the Irish language wasn't invented just to infuriate people forced to learn it at school. It was invented to do the same job as every other language, to bring people together so they could build villages and share food and have sex with each other, and shout 'Oh no, the Vikings are coming!' when the Vikings appeared, and all the other basic things that languages are invented to do.

It just so happened that the language those early Irish people invented was grammatically quite... emmm, complex, let's say, with awkward declensions and genitive cases and letters suddenly appearing in words for no reason, and h's making other letters completely disappear. And then later when people were trying to work out how to teach it, they seemed to go 'D'you know what 4–18 year olds LOVE? They love awkward declensions and gentive cases and letters that appear in words for seemingly no reason, so let's teach all that.'

When struggling through the subject at school, the most commonly heard complaint was that, sure, you'd never use it later in life; and that this was time that could be better spent mastering French and German so we could all move to Paris and become international business people. It turned out very few of us moved to Paris with our Leaving Cert French and ended up laughing as we drove a sports car through the 19th *arrondissement*. Besides, most of French class was spent writing and rewriting the same form letter, informing the family you are staying with that you will be arriving at the nearby train station at 3pm on Saturday and thanking them for collecting you. To all those who complain about the 'uselessness' of Irish, I have never had to actually write that letter to a French family, or indeed anyone else.

When you're at the chalkface, though, it's easy to forget that Irish is a language, not just a subject. I was brought up through Irish, and attended an All-Irish school, and have spoken the language almost every day of my life; but even I had to take a few years out of secondary school before I could shake off the sense of dread, and of unlearnt poetry about the Aran Islands, associated with Irish.

At some point in my mid-twenties, though, that ill-feeling suddenly fell away and I realised that, almost despite my best efforts, I had been gifted a rich inheiritance.

We sometimes forget that the purpose of learning isn't just utility in the workplace; and the benefits of a complex language are that the ideas it contains can be rich and poetic and profound and the stories it tells are ancient and essential. The Irish language is the key to unlocking the origin myth of the Irish people, and if there is one defining trait of the Irish people, it's that we love a good myth about ourselves.

And, ultimately, some of the words are just... better than their translations. I live in the UK where I lament daily that they have no word as good as 'leamh', or 'gruama', or 'ragairneacht'; because 'meh', 'grim' and 'bantz' don't really cut it.

You'll find your own favourites here, new ones too, and hopefully it'll leave you enjoying the language for its many subtle treasures.

Most of all though, enjoy the journey. There's no exam at the end.

Dara Ó Briain
July 2017

INTRODUCTION

In a way, children and adults are from different countries. There's a first word, then a second, and toddlers stumble and muddle their way through the language they receive as they try to find their way in this strange world in which they've landed. Then they find out that the word they've been using for a food or a body part isn't the 'real' word, and they realize that the people they call Mummy and Daddy have different names that they are called in the world outside the house. Words aren't just square blocks to fit in square holes anymore; some of them are a bit more like playdough.

I was born in a house full of books, so I always feel most at home when I'm surrounded by them. My dad had amassed a collection of titles that occupied every vertical surface in our home, covering every conceivable topic and written in an array of languages. As a small boy, I was convinced that I had found a collection of magic spells in my dad's library. It had been written in letters that I did not recognize from the alphabet I had seen in school. Was my dad a wizard?

It turned out he wasn't. The work in question was Dinneen's Dictionary, an early twentieth-century Irish-English lexicon beloved by Irish speakers. Like Dr Johnson's dictionary from over a century earlier, it is seen more as a relic than a practical reference – it's full of whimsical definitions and very unacademic subjectivity. However, like a debut album recorded in a garage by a band who would eventually become rock stars, its lack of polish and haphazard energy make it even more cherished than the slicker, more professional releases that succeeded it.

Another book Dad had in his collection was *Jimín Mháire Thaidhg*, from which he would read to my brothers and me at bedtime. It's a story of a boy growing up in West Kerry, getting himself into all sorts of trouble and surrounded by a slew of larger-than-life characters. It was a favourite of ours, and when I saw it in a bookshop in Dingle one summer, I had to have it. Reading it by myself turned out to be a massive disappointment; some clown had taken all the good bits out! Also, the words just didn't seem to have the same panache; they weren't wrong, but they plainly weren't right.

I complained to Dad about this, and he explained to me that he was reading to us from the Irish text, but translating it on the hop. Sometimes the Irish words and the English words weren't exactly the same, and two people could come to a different decision about their true meaning. As for the best bits, that was just prudish censorship.

Dad spoke about seven languages well,* and had a working understanding of several more.† He explained to me that languages had their own rules and internal logics, and that the

---

* English, Irish, French, Spanish, Latin, Japanese and German.

† Russian, Italian, Portuguese, Flemish and Greek – he even tried to learn Chinese in his eighties.

language you spoke could shape the way you thought without you even realizing it. A term like 'sister-in-law' could confusingly refer to the wife of his brother or his mam's sister; these different relationships had their own names in some languages but not in English. He told me jokes that had puns in English but that made no sense in French or Spanish. An idea was like liquid and languages were like differently shaped glasses; the liquid would take the shape of whatever glass it was poured into.

My spoken Irish had been fine in primary school, although I never really had a teacher who made it as interesting as my dad did. The self-consciousness of puberty gave me a long queue of things to feel awkward about – my lack of sporting prowess, my big ears, my inability to make small talk... and my big, long, unpronounceable name.‡ It was 1990, and the world was changing. Soccer had suddenly become very important, eclipsing Gaelic football – the very act of qualifying for the World Cup, let alone making the quarter-finals, left an indelible mark on the way Irish people saw themselves and their place in the world. A few short months later, the Republic elected its first female president, Mary Robinson, who epitomized a new, modern direction for politics, followed shortly by the revelation that a bishop had a son, scandalizing a nation. Irish was associated with an old Ireland, one that was being left behind by a shiny new world which lumped the language in (unfairly, in my hindsight-enhanced view)

‡ It's pronounced 'O Shay' – the gh and dh are silent.

•

§ In the eyes of some.

with extreme Republicanism, Catholicism and anti-British sentiment. An Irish name was seen as a marker that identified its carrier as a troublemaker, an advocate of unpopular views. A surname spelled *as Gaeilge* occupied the unhappy middle overlap in a Venn diagram whose circles included IRA foot soldiers, arriviste southsiders, strict teachers and unsuccessful creative types. Parents were concerned that schools should better prepare their children for inevitable emigration by teaching them something else. In a way that I hadn't noticed in the '80s, the Irish language was suddenly fair game for a slagging.

I drifted away from Irish as a teenager and I suspected that it didn't miss me. I loved going to the Gaeltacht,* mostly because of the opportunity to meet girls and get a respite from my parents, who had gone from being my dearest confidantes to the least cool people in the world in the time it took for my voice to break. But my negative attitude to Irish hurt my parents and my family's tradition of education. I remember grabbing Dad's copy of *Dinneen* in my teens out of boredom (I think I was looking for a cool word to smarten up an essay I was writing) and seeing that he had kept letters (in Irish) between Mam and himself from their courtship. That's touching to me now, but at the time I deemed it gross. Irish belonged to someone else, it seemed.

* Gaeltacht refers to those parts of Ireland where Irish is spoken as a first language, as well as to the summer schools run in those areas for teenagers to improve their Irish.

Days are long, but years are short. Fast forward to my thirties, a time when I had to come to terms with the fact that Dad, for all his fine qualities, was not immortal. He was falling more and visits to the hospital were lasting longer and getting more frequent. I had allowed myself to think that a lot of this was just maintenance, and it never actually occurred to me that our time together was running out. In 2014, when Dad wasn't well enough to make a speech at my wedding, I realized that I'd been completely in denial about how fragile he now was. When I returned from my honeymoon I took a serious interest in trying to learn more of the things he was passionate about so I could understand him better, especially his love of Irish.

I'm sure when my dad and his peers were children dreaming of the early twenty-first century, they imagined hover cars, robot butlers and postmen with jetpacks. Instead, we had a revolution in communications technology, especially social networking. Like most people old enough to remember the Second World War,† he was suspicious of the amount of personal information being stored centrally and how it might be used. However, the ability to communicate at the touch of a button – for free – with my brothers who had emigrated bowled him over, as did instant access to beloved French radio stations, old documentaries, census records from around the world... and the chance to wander down the never-forgotten streets of his old university quarter in Dijon through the magic of Google Maps.

† Or the Emergency, as it was charmingly known here.

Dad told me that his family had the first radio in their town and that people used to gather around to listen to GAA matches on a Sunday. In addition to the camaraderie, with the enjoyment of the match punctuated by droll observations, brief political rants and the occasional quarrel, he remembered two things about these get-togethers particularly well. Firstly, the poetic descriptions of the matches – sometimes alternating between English and Irish – were often contradicted on Monday afternoon by neighbours who had actually seen the game with their own eyes. Secondly, the new technology of the wireless radio allowed Dad and his brother to play practical jokes; they'd pretend it was turned on and then one of them, from behind a wall, would read out fake news about local people in an exaggerated RTÉ* accent.

I told Dad about how, although many of my dearest friends had emigrated and quite a few of those still in Ireland worked hours that prohibited traditional socializing, the camaraderie and craic he described did exist on Twitter timelines – friends enjoying a match or televised event together, with exchanges punctuated by droll observations, brief political rants and the occasional quarrel. There were exaggerated poetic descriptions of things too, and opportunities to tease and prank were rarely let lie.

* Raidió Teilifís Éireann (usually abbreviated to RTÉ) is Ireland's state broadcaster.

It occurred to us both, possibly at the same moment, that when humans were presented with a new way of communicating, often the first instinct was to have fun, to tease, to show off, to exaggerate and, most importantly, to share. The restrictions of a new medium (whether wireless radio or Twitter) were no more constraining than iambic pentameter or another poetic form; they were kindling to creative possibilities. The instinct to delight was innate; rules and pedantry were learned.

Of course, not everyone thinks of social networking as benevolently as I do, and I saw an overlap between how Twitter and the Irish language were perceived: angry little communities (allegedly) secluded from the serious concerns of the real world, things that wouldn't be missed. I couldn't shake off the idea that some sort of possibility was tucked away in this shared lack of prestige.

Hastily, tentatively and possibly prematurely, I set up an account called @theirishfor.

I set myself three rules for running this account:

1. Don't get involved in debates about state policy on Irish language – teaching, signage, constitutional controversy, expenditure and so on. Not because I don't have opinions – far from it. Simply because there's so much that's beautiful and fascinating to talk about but which never gets a look-in because of these debates. The Irish language doesn't belong to any government or party and its many charms exist whether it is promoted correctly or not.

2. It must be pleasing to those with no Irish, as well as to those with more than myself.

3. Build a palace from the rubble of everyone else's smashed expectations. People who expect the Irish language to be confined to things they aren't interested in talking about – smash their expectation. People who think that Irish doesn't belong to them – tear that thought down. People who say they can't remember a word of it – surprise them.

I wouldn't say that @theirishfor was an overnight success. It took almost three months before national media took notice, and then things were never quite the same again.

This isn't a schoolbook; I'm not a teacher and I can't promise that you'll be able to speak Irish by the time you get to the last page.* Try to imagine it as a fashion show of words, or a playground of language. There's some amazing buried treasure in this language of ours and stifling attitudes have kept it airtight and perfectly fresh for your consumption. Turn the page and see for yourself.

* Unless you already can – in which case, I'm unlikely to make you forget.

IRISH NAMES

or,

'How's That, Like, Pronounced?'

The story of the rise, fall and spread of languages is one of power. Like the rings inside a tree or the shape of a mountain, an area's language tells a story of destruction and growth, even when it isn't doing so explicitly. This is especially true of names. People name things they own or control – their kids, their pets, their property, etc. When you join a school, a team or a military regiment, you get a nickname to show you truly belong, assuring you that you are different from those outside the group.

An exonym is a name for something, especially a place, given to it by outsiders. English people don't describe themselves as 'Poms', Americans from states warmer than Alaska don't describe their homeland as the 'Lower 48' and Dublin people certainly don't refer to each other as 'Jackeens'. Correspondingly, an endonym would be a word that people from within a shared space used for each other. 'That's our word.' These boundaries between the exo and the endo can be blurry in a postcolonial, multilingual society, especially when it comes to the act of naming a child.

Picking a name for a brand new human being is a tricky business and a grave responsibility, with many competing considerations. What impact will the name have on the thousands of first impressions that child will make in life? What tribal and class loyalties will be declared or concealed? There are parents who want to acknowledge their child's Irish heritage with the name they pick, but only want to go so far. Traditional Irish names can be popular, but it's worth being forewarned before inflicting such a moniker on an innocent, defenceless child. Other parents are searching for a name that's unique – uniquely pretty, uniquely memorable, uniquely Irish.

For most of the inhabitants of the planet, Irish names are the only contact they'll ever have with the Irish language, so names contribute to the language's reputation as being beautiful but difficult. Some locations around Ireland (Clare, Kerry, Shannon, Tyrone and Derry) have become popular as given names, as has Erin, the name for Ireland itself. However, it is the names in the Irish language that the wider world is most likely to be familiar with, so I think they're a good base from which to explain how we pronounce Irish words in general.

Rather than kowtowing to expectation by putting names in alphabetical order or gender groupings, I've decided to list them based on how likely they are to be mispronounced and why. Hopefully this will be a good way to show you how to pronounce the Irish words in the rest of the book.

⅄ Tutorial Mode: The Easiest Names ⅄

The following names are pronounced just the way they look.

Ronan (m) This boy's name is derived from little seal (*rón*). As with a lot of the most popular names, a version without the fadas that were present in the original Irish (*Rónán*) has become more widespread. More on those fadas and how they inform pronunciation below.

Finbarr (m) The boy's name Finbarr has its critics, but it shares the honour of being the least mispronounced Irish name ever, along with Fintan. Finbarr is the patron saint of Cork, and the name is particularly popular there.

Fintan (m) Fintan rhymes with Tintin,* and many are the Fintans who endured this nickname in school. Just because your name is easy to pronounce doesn't mean you're out of the woods yet! It's suggested that this name means fair-haired or white fire.

> * As it is uttered in English; in Hergé's original French it'd sound more like 'Tantan'. Fintan does not rhyme with Tantan.

Colm (m) Colm can mean a dove or a pigeon . . . or a scar. Yes, a scarred dove would be *colm colmnach*. Irish doesn't use a **K**, so a **C** is always a hard **C**.

Nuala (f) Nuala isn't hard to pronounce; it's often taken as the abbreviation of Fionnuala, which is itself the simplified spelling of Fionnghuala (fair-shouldered). This gives a clue as to why some people may choose to use a trickier spelling; *fionn-ghuala* is an accurate reflection of what the name truly means, while Nuala more closely resembles Irish words with which it has no true etymological connection (like *nua*, new).

Colin (m) This has a hard **C**. The two most famous bearers of this name (at the time of writing) are former US Secretary of State Colin Powell and Dublin actor/former hellraiser Colin Farrell, both of whom use different pronunciations: *coe* (rhymes with oh!) *lin* and *coll* (rhymes with doll) *in*. The second version is the one used in Ireland. As for the first version, allowances need to be made for accents.

Aidan (m) This boy's name has been common in Ireland for years but has become a lot more popular in the States and further afield since the '00s, thanks to the character playing one of Carrie's more likeable suitors in *Sex and the City*.

Ciara (f) Another hard **C** – *key-ra*. It never occurred to me that this was a hard one to get your tongue around, but '00s singer Ciara pronounced it *see-are-ah*. The spelling used by English actress Kiera Knightly is very rare in Ireland, but may have been influenced by the divergent spellings of the male version of this name . . .

Ciarán (m) The male version of Ciara. I haven't heard of a male R&B singer called *see-are-ahn* yet, but there's still time. Some people prefer to spell this name Kieran, which illustrates the difference between the two A's, with and without a *fada*.

Conor (m) Rhymes with honour, or 'honor' as they spell it in the United States (the English language is not innocent of heterogeneous pronunciation and divergent spelling).

Aifric (f) This girl's name is pronounced like the continent Africa without the final A. The etymology of this name is shrouded in mystery. It's been suggested that it's derived from *aifreann* (Mass) or Africa (although why Africa would be considered as a subject for a name in Ireland at a time when foreign place names gener-

ally weren't, would need to be explained). Either way, today it's best known as the main character in TG4's* *Aifric*, a show for kids about a Dublin girl whose family move to the Gaeltacht.

* Teilifís na Gaeilge (TG4) is Ireland's bilingual television station; it's original programming made in Irish.

Ruairí (m) There are more than a few Irish names with a multiplicity of spelling options. Generally, the spelling of boys' names is a bit more stable than that of girls' names, although Rory/Ruairí/Ruaidhrí co-exist peacefully. That name means red-haired king – *rua* and *rí*.

Conall (m) The Irish for Donegal is *Tír Conall* – Conall's land. As with Conor, Ciaran, Ciara and Colm, it's got a hard **C**.

Lochlann (*m*) *Lochlannach* means Viking, Scandinavian† or pirate. This is the origin of the boy's name Lochlann (and its variations). It should not be confused with *lachnach*, an adjective to describe a place with many ducks. One of the names in Irish for a pirate is *foghlaí mara*, which translates literally as sea trespasser.‡

† A *Dubh-Lochlannach* (dark Viking) is a Dane and a *Fionn-Lochlannach* (fair Viking) is a Norwegian.

‡ The Jolly Roger is *an brat dubh,* which translates literally as the black cloak/mantle/curtain.

Another Irish term for pirate is *uiging*, which comes from Danish (viking) and is the origin of the surname Higgins.

The **ch** in Lochlann is nothing to fear; it's pronounced much the same as Christmas. This is also true in other names...

Fiachra (m) Fiachra sounds a lot like *fiacla*, the Irish word for teeth (and the name of a once-popular toothpaste brand) so 'Teeth' was a go-to nickname for lads with this first name. *Fiach* can mean a single tooth or a raven, and is also a popular boy's name in its own right.

Darach (m) My own first name is still quite niche, but it doesn't make unreasonable demands of the pronouncer. The first syllable rhymes with far, the second with Bach.* However, when people see it and recognize it as an Irish name, they assume it mustn't be pronounced the way that it looks – I've heard Daritch, Dalek, Darth and (most frequently) Dara. Darach means like an oak tree. Having an unusual name means you get very excited when anyone else with the same name turns up; imagine my glee when the evil wizard in the TV show *Teen Wolf* was also called Darach.

* Catholic composer Johann Sebastian Bach, who was father to twenty-four children.

Dara/Daire/Darragh (both) These come from the Irish word for oak tree too. So why is it a different name you ask? The same reason that Iain, Euan, Owen, John, Jon and Nathan are all derived from Jonathan. Dara and Daire are increasingly popular as names for girls (I haven't heard of a girl called Darragh yet).

ᚤ ᚤ ᚤ ᚤ ᚤ Fun with Fadas ᚤ ᚤ ᚤ ᚤ ᚤ

Conán (m) Remember Ronan? Remember how easy that was to pronounce? Doesn't Conán look like Ronan? Aye, but there's a wee hat on that A. If you're familiar with US TV host Conan O'Brien and you know how his name is pronounced, this is close, but that little hat on the **A** changes it a little. It's called a *fada*, which means long in Irish. A *fada* on a vowel makes it long. So Conan is pronounced *co-nawn*. It's a great name, meaning wolf.

Gráinne (f) This was a hugely popular name for girls born between the 1960s and early 1990s. Girls with this name would often be hilariously nicknamed *granna* (which means ugly), but I'm pleased to confirm that this is not the origin of the name – the *fada* makes that quite clear. Gráinne means a grain, and it's been conjectured that the name might have its ultimate root in the name of a crop goddess; however, this is secondary to the name's myth-ological resonance from the popular *Tóraíocht Dhiarmada agus Ghráinne* and the legendary pirate queen Gráinne Maol (bald Gráinne, on account of her shaved head). The Irish for hedgehog is *gráinneog* – young Gráinne or little grain. A person or entity with hedgehog-like qualities (defensive, adorable, spiky-haired or stressed by traffic) might be described as *gráinneogach*. There's no word for this in English, although I'm told it's *igelqualitäten* in German.

Éamonn/Éamon (m) If you have studied French, you'll be comforted to know that an **É** in Irish behaves much like an **É** in French – *enchanté, café, je suis desolé*. So Éamon rhymes with 'hey, mon'. This was once a hugely popular boy's name (possibly on account of Mr de Valera*) but has slid out of the charts in recent years (possibly on account of Mr de Valera).

Realtín (f) A lot of girl's names end with **-ín**, much the same as female names in Romance languages end with an A. The suffix **-ín** is pronounced *een*, rhyming with clean, bean or tangerine. This gorgeous name means little star.

Cailín (f) This is the Irish word for a girl; it's more popular as a name among families of Irish heritage abroad than it is in Ireland. Thus, it's often spelled Colleen, which is a fair reflection of how it is uttered.

Ríona (f) This can be an abbreviation of Caitríona or Lasairíona, but also stands as a name in its own right and is derived from Ríon, a queen† or noble lady. *Ree-uh-nah*.

Oscar/Óran (m) The Irish boy's name Oscar is not pronounced like the award; it rhymes with busker. An accentless **O** is really more of an *'uh'* sound, whereas **Ó** sounds like *'oh'*. The easy way to remember this is to think of every classic Irish surname – O'Reilly, O'Callaghan, O'Shea, etc. – and remember each **O** is really an **Ó** that's been anglicized.

* Éamon de Valera (1882–1975), TD for Clare, second Taoiseach and third President of the Republic of Ireland, President of the League of Nations, American passport-holder and maths teacher.

† The go-to words for queen in Irish are *banrí*, or just *rí* if you prefer using a gender-neutral term for monarch.

Úna (f) You may have seen the name Oona (or Oonagh, which combines the Anglicization of **Ú** with a silent gh for some reason). That **Ú** is indeed pronounced like an *ooh*.

ᛉ ᛉ ᛉ ᛉ ᛉ ᛉ **Normal Names** ᛉ ᛉ ᛉ ᛉ ᛉ ᛉ

Sometimes a celebrity or colleague has a baby and they give their child a name that shows a lack of self-awareness, a hint of pretension, a dearth of consideration . . . in other words, 'notions'. While a blind eye can be turned to corruption, any hint of affectation in Ireland must be stamped out early and often. The following names, although they include a point of difference between English and Irish pronunciation, have been categorized as normal – their authenticity has been verified and they are sufficiently popular to avoid accusations of notions. Speaking of notions . . .

Aisling (f) As well as meaning 'vision in a dream' and being a very popular girl's name, Aisling has become slang for an overly-sensible young country woman with conservative tastes and a strong aversion to notions; the kind who works in Dublin and returns to her home village religiously every Friday evening. This usage has been promulgated in the cult Facebook group *'Oh My God What a Complete Aisling'* (or OMGWACA as its members sometimes call it for short).

Aislingeach means dreamy, romantic or quixotic (although quixotic is a word reeking of notions). *Aisfhreagra* means backchat. This isn't, to my knowledge, connected to the name Aisling (although notions may invoke *aisfhreagraí*).

⋎⋎⋎⋎⋎⋎ **The Letter S** ⋎⋎⋎⋎⋎⋎

Aisling is mostly compatible with the phonetic expectations of Anglophones, except for that s, which sounds more like an '*sh*': *ash-ling*. This is normal in Irish, and you'll find the following names all enjoy a '*sh*' sound where you see an **S/s**:

Sean (m) You're probably so used to this one that you can't remember ever wondering how it was pronounced. Seán is the true Irish spelling, as *sean* means old.

Siobhán (f) *Shove on.* More on that **bh** that sounds like a '*v*' below.

Oisín (m) How would a Cockney bloke say hush? '*Ush*', of course. *Ush-een.* This popular name means a fawn or young deer and is the name of the main character in one of the best-loved stories in Irish mythology.

Sinéad (f) *Shin-aid.* Even though this is the name of one of Ireland's most famous singers, this still gets mispronounced.

Siún (f) *Shoe-in.* The Donegal version of Siobhán, recently increasing in popularity in the other thirty-one counties.

Róisín (f) *Roe-sheen.* Little rose.

Eilís (f) *Eye-leash.* This name is given as the translation of both Alice and Elizabeth.

Siofra (f) *She-frah.* Elf/fairy.

There are some that break the rule, of course (rules are usually simple, it's the exceptions that make them hard).

Sorcha (f) *Circa* and *Sore-ha* are both widely-accepted pronunciations of this name, which is taken as the Irish translation of Sarah.

Saoirse (f) Freedom! Pronounced *Sir-shah*.

Aonghus (m) An **s** at the end of a word is pronounced much like an **s** in English. *Aon* (rhymes with lane) and *gus* (rhymes with bus).

Seamus (m) *Shame-us* – rhymes with famous. Like Aonghus, the final **s** is sibilant. The first **S** is treated like Seán, Sinéad and Siobhán.

Órla (f) This one has a variety of accepted spellings in common use – Orla, Órla, Órlaith, Órfhlaith, Orlagh and so on. Just one thing though: a squirt of vomit is *sconnóg orla* in Irish. That's right, not only is Orla a girl's name, it can also mean vomit. I should probably clarify that the girl's name Orla is actually derived from Órfhlaith and means golden princess. Not vomit. *Brúcht, sceith* and especially *urlacan* are words for vomit that won't annoy all the cool Orlas out there.

Two points about pronunciation here. As Órla and Orla have significantly different meanings (when used in Irish: the dropping of *fadas* with Irish names in English is an inevitable compromise), you'd reasonably expect them to sound different.

Second point – Órla is a simplified spelling of

Órfhlaith, because the **fh** is silent and the ith is more like an **h** in English. I discuss this in more detail later.

Emer (f) Like Órla, Emer (the name of Cúchulainn's* wife) is subject to a range of accepted spellings – Émer, Eimear, Eimer and so on. They are all pronounced *e-mer* (rhyming with screamer, steamer or schemer). Contemporary scholars now say that this name should have actually been pronounced *ever* all along, but I don't see that catching on at this stage.

* Cúchulainn is a major character in Irish mythology, who I'll be discussing in more detail later.

Deirdre (f) *Deirdre of the Sorrows* is a story from Irish mythology (popularized by Lady Gregory and J. M. Synge) that doesn't end very well for anyone involved, as the name suggests. Speaking of not ending well, sometimes this fine name is spoken aloud as *dear-dree*, a sound that doesn't obey English or Irish pronunciation rules; it's actually more like *dear-drah*. That unaccented **e** at the end makes a short *eh* sound.

Cait/Caitríona (f) The **it** in Cait (and Caitríona too) is pronounced like the **ch** in charming or chunky. Readers of a certain age will remember that Cait was the narrator's best friend in the beloved schoolbook *Peig*.† With its accented and unaccented **i**'s next to each other, Caitríona is a good reference point to use if you're reading a new Irish word with an I and need to know how it sounds.

† *Peig*'s unpopularity, so long a synecdoche for the failures of the Irish-language movement and state policy, has become a cliché in itself.

ᚩ ᚩ ᚩ ᚩ ᚩ Invisible V Names ᚩ ᚩ ᚩ ᚩ ᚩ

These names are still mainstream, but they have a '*v*' sound without actually having the letter v. This causes confusion in other countries for some reasons. Why do so many letter combinations sound like **v**? Why can't they just be replaced with a letter **v**? It's not as if modern Irish has a zero-tolerance policy on the letter **v** anymore (*tvúit, vótáil, de Valera*).

The best analogy I can give here is a musical one. Take a perfectly tuned guitar and play a note on the sixth string. Go to the fifth string, press on the fifth fret; you'll play the same note. Likewise, with the fourth string and the tenth fret, and so on. **Bh** and **mh** are like the same note played on different strings.

'mh'

Caoimhe (f) This name is sometimes anglicized as Keeva, which is a fair reflection of how it sounds (although Gaeltacht natives put a twirl in the -aoi that is hard to replicate).

Niamh (f) This very popular moniker means bright/brightness and is the name of the girl who came from Tír na nÓg‡ to win young Oisín's heart in the beloved tale. The popularity of this story might explain why the spelling of this name (and Oisín too) have not

‡ *Tír* means land or country, and poetically sounds a bit like the English word tear (liquid sadness, not damaged clothing). Tír na nÓg is the land of eternal youth in Irish mythology; it is not the afterlife but visitors are warned never to come back once they decide to leave. The enduring popularity of this story might be due to this resonant analogy with Irish emigration, as well as the Freudian fear of marriage changing a man and taking him away from his mammy/mates.

diverged as much as other Irish names whose pronunciation is incompatible with Anglo sensibilities.

'bh'

Ailbhe (f) This sounds a bit like Elva, and comes from an old word for white.

Beibhín (f) *Bay-veen*. This girl's name means beautiful, blonde woman (*bé* and *fionn*); some say it originally referred to Viking women (which sounds plausible), but others point out that this was the name of notorious Viking-basher Brian Boru's mother.

⸜ H is for Hush – the Silent Letters ⸝

Sometimes a friend from overseas makes a valiant effort pronouncing an Irish name, only to find out that the string of consecutive consonants is actually skipped over completely. While this should be a relief – it's easier than it looks – the reaction is often exasperation or bemusement. What's the point of having letters you don't say?

Personally, I have a sentimental weakness for silent letters; they remind us that there's more to the world than the bits that are heard. Silent letters, if you'll listen to them, will tell you a story of a word's history, and give clues as to how a word will change in different grammatical circumstances. They don't shout, but they point the way and nudge things forward.

Let's talk about **gh**, **fh**, **dh**, **bh** and **aith**.

Seamus Heaney used the silent gh as a kind of shibboleth and a signifier for English confusion about the internal complexities of Ireland in his poem 'Broagh': 'in Broagh/ its low tattoo/among the windy boor trees/and rhubarb blades/ended almost/suddenly, like that last/gh the strangers found/difficult to manage'.

We've mentioned Órlagh and Fionnghuala. There's also:

Bronagh (f) *Bro-na*. While this is most commonly spelled without a fada, it is derived from *brón*, meaning sad.

Clodagh (f) *Clow-da*. The original Clodagh was a river goddess.

Oonagh (f) *Ooh!-na*. An alternative spelling of Úna.

Caragh (f) *Cah-rah*

Muirgheal (f) 'You're terrible, Muriel!'

Ríoghnach (f) *Ree-an-och*. This means royal or queen.

Donagh (m) Yes, the silent **gh** can haunt boys' names too.

Darragh (m) Sounds just like Dara.

Maghnus (m) *Man-us*. This is my younger brother's name and he's suffered the indignity of being called Magnus by people with silent **gh**'s in their own names.

'fh'

If you see an fh in Irish, it's asleep . . . so just tiptoe past it.

Lasairfhíona (f) This gorgeous name, as a poetic metaphor for inspiration, means flame of wine: *lasair* is a flame, *fíon* is wine. When you're making a combined word form like this, the second noun is in the genitive case (*an fhíona* – the **h** silences the **f**). So this name would be pronounced *lah-sa-rhee-na*. The spelling Lasairíona is also popular (especially in my house, as it's my daughter's name).

Caoilfhionn (f) Sometimes this one gets anglicized as Keelin. No Caoilfhionn has ever walked out of a Starbucks with her name spelled correctly on her coffee cup. Like Lasairfhíona, Caoilfhionn is a compound form; *caol*, slim and *fionn*, fair.

'db' and 'dhbh'

The bh, as we've seen, sounds like a v. The dh is like a whispered y (*O mo Dhia* – the Irish for 'Oh my God' – sounds like 'O muh Ye-ah'). Therefore, a dhbh most closely resembled a 'yv' or 'eve' sound in English. In some names this will be presented as db; allow me to explain why.

Medb (f) Like Órla and Emer, this name (meaning she who intoxicates) presents itself with numerous canonical spelling options. The two most famous are Queen Medb (the intensely single-minded ruler from mythology, Cúchulainn's worthy foe) and Maeve Binchy (the writer known for her cosy fiction, but also her mercilessly witty journalism). In addition to these two spellings, it also turns up as Medhbh, Méabh, Maedhbh, Maebh and so forth. This diversification gives an insight into changes in Irish spelling conventions over time.

Up until the '50s, the d and b would've had an accent called a *ponc seimhithe* (represented by a little dot on top). Modern spelling conventions introduced along with the

Hidden Level

Aodh (*m*) This one (often anglicized as Hugh) is a bit cheeky; the **dh** is silent so it sounds a bit like '*eh*'.

Muireann (*f*) In the extraordinary TV show *Catastrophe*, Sharon Horgan's character names her daughter Muireann, to the horror of the British and American characters who can't quite manage to pronounce it. There are no silent letters here, but there's a little flourish to pronouncing the '**mui**'; it's almost like the exaggerated kissing sound that glamorous Hollywood women used to make – 'mwah, mwah, dahling!' So try pronouncing it '*mweh-rehn*'. The same '*mwu*' sound is present in names like Muiris and Muirchertach.

Doireann (*f*) Sometimes people ask me to spell out Irish words phonetically, and one of the reasons I'm reluctant to do so is that I see a name like Doireann and I struggle to think of how anyone could get it wrong. It just seems obvious to me that this rhymes with *stir-in*.

1959 English-Irish dictionary replaced this handy grammatical feature with a letter h after the accented letter. Versions of names already in common use before this decision was made – like Medb and Sadb – have survived without the inclusion of the h. Names that spiked in popularity in the '60s and '70s weren't affected by the conflict of an old spelling and a new spelling, and are typically more stable.

Contrary to what you might have expected, Irish language names were not very widespread in the first half of the twentieth century; the prevailing opinion in the Catholic Church was that saints' names (in English) were preferable to pagan ones (in Irish) and this view was enforced at the baptismal font.* My dad, Domhnall, was christened Daniel because of such an insistence. Patrick, Mary, Mick, Bernadette, Carmel and Marian are examples of names entrenched in Irish communities, without an origin in the language, that flourished during this practice. Irish names deemed worthy for a priest to 'pour water on' at the time often had a particular local resonance – like Sadhbh.

* This was a widespread practice rather than an infallible doctrine, and some priests were stricter than others. It was especially prevalent in the early years of the Free State when the clergy were still antipathetic to Irish independence.

Sadb/Sadhbh (f) Which brings us to *Sive* – the John B. Keane play takes its name from the phonetic spelling of Sadb/Sadhbh. Historically, this was a particularly popular name in Kerry, where the town of Cahirsiveen (*Cathair Saidhbhín* – 'little Sadb's fort') is to be found. This must be the Irish name that gets the most frequent incredulity from Americans, Australians and baristas; if not, it can't be far from the top. Just as the mythological character Sadhbh changed from a doe to a beautiful woman, the spelling of the name has changed form into the guise of Saibh, Saeve and even Sabhbh.

ＹＹＹ   End-Level Boss Names   ＹＹＹ

By now you've covered the biggest pronunciation pit-falls, problems and peccadillos that pop up in Irish. They weren't as hard as you thought. But, like in an old arcade game, there's always a big bad one, the kind you have to defeat before you get to the next level – the end-level boss.

These names are either intimidatingly spelled or counter-intuitively pronounced, but once you know how to beat them, they'll never intimidate you again. When you were taught to drive, you learnt how to change gears, use the handbrake and reverse in different lessons, but as a qualified driver you use all three techniques together instinctively.

Conchubar (m) This is pronounced '*Conor*' and I will concede that it doesn't really look like that. This is the old Irish spelling used in the *Táin*† for the king of Ulster's name, and the popularity of that text explains how this spelling has retained (some) popularity.‡

† The *Táin* is the centrepiece of Irish mythology, the epic poem which discusses events precipitated by an argument between Medb and her husband, King Ailill, over which one of them 'married up' (who was richer). Medb's auditors conclude that she is poorer by one prize bull, and she undertakes to obtain a suitable animal. This brings her into conflict with Cúchulainn, the James Bond of the Iron Age. It doesn't end well.

‡ A translation of the *Táin* by poet Thomas Kinsella, illustrated by Louis le Brocquy, was published in 1969, arriving at a moment when popular culture was open to mythology and mysticism, but also coinciding with the Civil Rights Movement in Northern Ireland. This translation (and its illustrations) became extremely popular and influential among creatives in many fields.

A Fada Can Make All the Difference

Éire	Ireland
Eire	a burden
Stáir	frenzy
Stair	history
Ríocht	kingdom
Riocht	disguise
Cráic	anus
Craic	mirth or merriment
Ábhann	tune or strain of music
Abhann	river
Fáil	destiny, capability
Fail	hiccup
Duán	fish hook
Duan	poem or song (of course a song could have a catchy hook . . .)
Fán	straying/wandering
Fan	stay
Céad	100 or first
Cead	permission (as in 'an bhfuil cead agam . . .')*
Brícín	peat briquette
Bricín	freckle
Dúchán	an inkwell or darkening
Dúchan	sadness
Mórbhéalach	big-mouthed
Mórbhealach	main road

* 'May I have permission' – the beginning of the most famous sentence in Irish, when children request leave from a teacher to use the bathroom.

† The spellings *Conchubar* and *Medb* owe their continued existence to the popularity of the *Táin*.

This example applies to some of the other 'harder' names; some names achieved popularity at different stages of the language's journey to standard spelling.†

Muirchertach (m) This was once a popular name (my grandfather bore it) but was routinely anglicized as Mortimer, even though there is no commonality of meaning. Mortimer comes from French and means dead (or still) sea, but Muirchertach (*mwer-chur-tock-h*) was the name of a high king of Ireland.

Faoiltighearna (f) This name was in *Irish Names and Surnames*, Reverend Patrick Wolfe's 1923 collection of popular names in Ireland; Ciara, Síofra and Realtín weren't. Where did all the Faoiltighearnas go? It's a great name, meaning wolf lady (*faol*, wolf and *tiarna*, lord/lady). *F-whale-tear-nah*.

Toirdhealbhach (m) In the twelfth century, Muirchertach Muimhnech was a prince in Connaught, son of the wonderfully named Toirdhealbhach. This is generally simplified to Turlough these days, which gives a clue to how the original name is pronounced – with a silent dh (like Aodh). *Tur-alvach*.

Flaithbertaigh (both) Remember how I told you that Orla is derived from Órflaith? Come on, it was only ten pages ago. Well, the **aith** here sounds much the same. This name has been simplified to Flaherty over the years, and is now more popular as a surname. It has been suggested that this can either mean bright leader or scheming leader.

Chaoilfhiaclaigh (m) By now, this should be no trouble to you. That quiet **fh** in the middle, just like Lasairfhíona or Caoilfhionn. A **ch** at the beginning, just like Christmas, and a final **aigh** like a contented sigh. *Chol-a-heek-lah*. This name was very nearly given to my brother. It's a compound form: *caol* (meaning slender or narrow, like Caoilfhionn above) and *fiacla* (meaning teeth) – narrow teeth.

See? Not that hard at all.

PRIMARY SCHOOL

The Irish for childhood is **leanbaíocht**... not to be confused with **lansaíocht**, which means fighting with lances.

There's a section in *Jimín Maire Thaidhg* by An Seabhac[*] where a teacher asks a class a mathematical question: if a horse can run four miles in an hour, how far will it run in twenty-four hours? Jimín, rather than merely multiplying the speed by the time, observes that twenty-four hours is a long journey, and wouldn't the horse need to stop for a rest or a feed, couldn't she get a stone in her shoe, what if the rider bumped into someone he knew on the way and had to catch up, and would they be taking the new road? Also, how much of a hurry was the fella in? Rather than take these concerns on board, the teacher gives Jimín a hiding (as was common at the time).

[*] Pádraig Ó Siochfhradha (1883–1964) – author, teacher, senator and Irish-language activist. His pen-name, *An Seabhac*, means the hawk. *Jimín* is his *Tom Sawyer*-esque novel about boyhood in Kerry.

This scene brings back memories for me of primary school – being at the mercy of adults for whom lessons were merely megaphones through which their own insecure authority could be broadcast. Not all of them, of course, but enough for it to cloud the water. A particular incident from Junior Infants* (the class we were in when we were five years old) sticks out in my mind. Myself and Michelle Whelan were brought to the front of the classroom, handed an ersatz clock by our teacher (for legal reasons, let's call her Fidelma Fox-Fagan) and told to move the hands to tell certain requested times. Michelle was told to do an easy one (a quarter past twelve) and duly obliged. When the clock was handed to me, I was asked to make the clock tell the time of twenty past three. However, by this point the arms had become loose (from all the yanking) and when I held the 'correct' time in front of me, the arms both slumped down to half past six. As the whole class laughed, my teacher advised me that I was a 'very stupid boy'; the more I tried to explain myself, the angrier she got.

* Junior Infants and Senior Infants are the amusingly-named grades in Ireland for five- and six-year-olds, right before they start First Class (equivalent to First Grade in America). Sometimes Senior Infants is called High Babies.

It was under the gentle tutelage of this kind woman that I was introduced to the Irish language.

The first passages we read in Irish involved **buachaillí bó** (cowboys) and **spásairí** (astronauts), because that's what five-year-olds were interested in at the time. When I was telling my parents about what I'd learnt at school, they were bemused that the Irish language passages dealt with things so removed from the experience of Irish-language communities. This confused me. If I was from Ireland, and was learning Irish in school, wasn't I a member of the Irish-language community? Why would one language not be good enough (or be too good) to tell the stories of certain kinds of people? Nonetheless, I buried these concerns and moved onwards with my studies. I enjoyed being told how intelligent I was by grown-ups, and school offered opportunities to have this itch scratched.

My next Irish language-related memory was that two boys in my class didn't have to study it, and could read to their heart's content while we beavered away. One of them had been born in Barcelona with a Catalan father, and was learning Spanish instead at the weekend. The other boy was from a family who were preparing to emigrate to Australia, and his father had insisted to the school that there was no point in him learning a language he wouldn't use there. The immigrant and the imminent emigrant were both marked out as not normal by their exclusion from the Irish language, and I can't help but feel that this marked the rest of us unconsciously. A few years later another boy was excluded from Irish lessons because of a medical condition – the euphemism at the time was that he 'had a hole in his heart' – and his classmates used to tease him about how lucky he was for being spared from Irish.

I went to Junior and Senior Infants at the convent school, at which point the class was split and the boys were sent to Saint Mary's on the Grange Road. There were children on my road who didn't go to the convent or to Saint Mary's; at the time, it never occurred to me that there was a connection between this and the fact that we'd never see them at

Mass. But other kids picked up on it; children with different religions went to different schools, and there must have been a reason for it.

For a lot of people from Ireland, the Irish words they remember or recognize remind them of childhood. This has led to lots of them becoming loanwords in English when something needs to be described in a twee or non-threatening way.

The following words would be good examples of this:

Madra	Dog. There's an apocryphal tale about Irish people in the United Kingdom believing that madras curry was made with dog meat on account of this word.
Luch	Mouse. A wet mouse would be **luch fliuch**, which is fun to say.
Cat	Cat (although the **a** is, as you now know, pronounced differently).
Muc	Pig. Easy to remember because pigs enjoy languishing in the muck.
Capall	Horse. The similarity to the onomatopoeic clip-clop in English made this easy to remember.
Múinteoir	Teacher. Humorously, **múin** can mean to teach or to pee (as a grammatical form of **mún**).

Teach — House. This, along with **fear** (man) and **bean** (woman), is one of the words that looks just like an unrelated English word.

Mílsean — Sweets

Uachtar reoite — Ice cream

Lámh — Hand (ideally with **mílsean** or **uachtar reoite** in it).

Gúna — Dress. When beloved '80s adventure film *The Goonies* was released, some of us were surprised that it had nothing to do with ball gowns and frocks.

Ciúnas — Silence. **Múinteoirí** got a lot of mileage out of this one.

Buachaill — Boy

Cailín — Girl

Bainne — Milk

Uisce — Water

Bóthar — Road. A little country road, especially one with a bit of grass growing in the middle, is a **bóithrín** (boreen/bohareen in English).

Lá — Day

Oíche — Night

Paistí — Children

Súgradh   Play. *Súgradh* was also the name of a wonderful magazine for kids that was circulated to us at school. Older readers would get *Siamsa* or *Solas*.

Seomra   Room

In the '80s, the jewel in the crown of First Class* in primary school was making your First Holy Communion – this meant you could finally get a wafer at Mass, but it also meant that you had to make confession. Before our First Confession, I remember a priest addressing the class, jogging our memory of things that we might not have thought of as sinful, but which were worth confessing. Choosing to wait until the end of *The A-Team* before setting the table for example, fighting with siblings and classmates or using rude words.

After confession, we'd compare penances to see who was the boldest boy in the class; I'd routinely be teased for only getting three Hail Marys and a Glory Be (Glory Be is the shortest prayer and is the penance equivalent of being put on a naughty step instead of getting a spanking). However, just like judges, some priests were harsher than others. One day, kids marched out of the confession box in horror when a visiting priest insisted on giving us our penances in Irish as well as English. I'm

* This has since been changed; Catholic kids now make their FHC in Second Class. They changed 'and also with you' to 'and with your spirit' too when I wasn't looking!

•

† The Gaelic League, *Conradh na Gaeilge* in Irish, was an organization set up in 1893 to revive use of the Irish language after the devastation caused by the Famine.

still not sure if he was trying to promote the use of Irish, or weaponize it.

As we knelt in church, praying our extra-long bilingual penances, some of us began to question the benefits of the language for the first time.

In spite of the perceived link in the memories of many, the Irish language movement and the Catholic Church were at odds with each other more often than not. The Gaelic League† was secular and diverse, 'pagan' Irish names were anglicized by the church to equivalent saints' names before a baptism and early Irish-language schools were consciously independent of diocesan scrutiny. In fact, the rise of the Gaelic League occurred at the same time as the cultivation of a new, respectable Catholic middle class who were unsentimental about the Irish language; centuries of historical antipathy between Catholicism and the British administration in Dublin Castle were discarded on account of mutual self-interest as the Jesuits‡, Holy Ghost Fathers, Carmelites and Cistercians established private schools to prepare Catholic boys for careers in the professions and the officer ranks of business, administration and the military§.

‡ Observers of Irish politics who struggle to see a difference between Fianna Fáil and Fine Gael should be directed to tribal loyalties rather than individual policies; typically, FF politicians were alumni of Christian Brothers' schools whereas the FG lads typically attended Jesuit schools – until the ascent of Enda Kenny.

§ As well as careers in the church, of course.

St Mary's was blessed to have on its staff one of the greatest primary school teachers in the world, a man called Fintan. A gentle giant with enormous hands (how he used his massive fingers to correctly play notes on the tin whistle was never answered), Fintan famously declared that no boy would leave his class without knowing how to boil an egg (whether it was on the curriculum or not) and would introduce children to classical music by playing it in the background when they were working away at sums or essays. His love of hurling, music and Greek mythology was as infectious as his sense of humour. If he had harboured dreams of treading the boards as a younger man, he hid them well, except when he'd read *The Odyssey* to an

Just because two words sound a bit similar, that isn't to say that their meanings overlap. That'd be wrong.

Eagla	fear
Eaglais	church
Ár nAthair	Our Father
An nathair	the snake
Aifreann	Mass
Ifreann	hell
Bíobla	Bible
Bíobha	enemy/wrongdoer
Naofacht	holiness
Saofacht	waywardness
Dobhriste	sacred
Fobhristí	underpants

enthralled classroom, performing every character with a combination of showmanship and psychological empathy that left a lasting impression.

Sadly, I never had Fintan as a teacher, although I could hear the laughter of his students from the room next door. My **múinteoir** was a gentleman who, for legal reasons, I will call Cavendish. Cavendish was an unhinged, homophobic, IRA sympathizer from Louth who saw classroom lessons as a chore to be endured in between PE lessons. Any child who wasn't sporty was alone. I was not sporty.

One of the things I absolutely loved in primary school was learning about mythology – especially Irish mythology. The adventures of Cúchulainn, especially his early years, were particular favourites. Greek and Roman history and mythology captivated me too; I couldn't get enough of stories about the Romans and their conquests and the quirks and traits of the various emperors. In an ill-advised moment of independent thinking, I concluded that there must be a time overlap between the events described in Irish mythology and Roman history.

'Sir, how come the Romans never came to Ireland?'

'They didn't think Ireland was worth the trouble, Darach.' This was an alarming thing to hear from a man like Cavendish who, even by the standards of the time, was sourly and defensively patriotic.

'But why not? Sure, aren't we great?'

'Because they thought it was worthless. They believed that it never stopped raining here. They called it the land of eternal winter – Hibernia.'

'But why didn't they call Iceland or Sweden Hibernia instead of us – surely they're much colder!'

'All I know is that Caesar once said he could capture the island with a single company, but it wouldn't even be worth that small effort.'

'But sir,' another boy piped up, 'if we weren't worth invading, why did the Brits invade us?'

The 'not-worth-invading' story slotted perfectly into the national inferiority complex that we were gradually absorbing. It dovetailed neatly with another story about the Romans that was popular at the time, the scene in *Life of Brian* when the protagonist asks what the Romans have ever done for them (when it turns out that there is an extensive list of things the Romans have done), a scene that was received at the time in Ireland as a pointed rebuke to ungrateful Republicans in Northern Ireland and struggling former colonies.

You really can't overstate the depth of anti-English feelings in Ireland at the time; the Troubles were raging up North, Irish jokes were a staple feature of light entertainment on British television, Irish celebrities were routinely claimed as British and Thatcher, Paisley and their respective entourages didn't need to be liked as much as their successors. Lots of our adult family members had anecdotes about bad experiences living in England (ranging from frustrating misunderstandings to outright hostility).* We picked up on it from a very young age. And yet... everyone had English cousins who weren't monsters. Everyone had family in one or more of the larger English cities, family who were generally doing well for themselves, often better than the family they left behind. Everybody's dad supported an English football club. Some of our friends had even… whisper it… been born over there.†

The various grievances accrued by Irish people in their own lifetimes and before can be judged on their own merits or as part of a whole culture or climate of disrespect; either way, it's worth considering the impact that harbouring anti-English sentiments had on Ireland, on Irish people and on the way issues of public interest were discussed.

One thing that suffered as a consequence was the Irish language, even though it was ostensibly promoted by its most passionate advocates. The theme of that promotion, however, was the language's constant peril. While the stories my dad read to us and the banter my parents would have with their friends in the Kerry Gaeltacht were warm, irreverent and musical, a lesson from Cavendish had a similar atmosphere to the examining of conscience before confession. The Irish language was in danger of extinction, but we wanted to listen to Michael Jackson albums and watch *MacGyver*. The Irish language was in peril, but we were too weak and couldn't stand up to a little peer pressure. In retrospect, it was pretty Orwellian the way teachers would accuse you of being a sheep if you didn't do what they said.

One day a boy called Darren mentioned that his dad had

* This wasn't the case when my mates and I were old enough to travel over on our own. One of the pleasant side-effects of the Peace Process was the Irish accent suddenly being considered sexy in the United Kingdom. When we were on a school trip to Stratford-upon-Avon in 1995, one older teacher compared this cultural shift to 'seeing a postman chase a dog down the road'.

† Such lads included Phil Lynott, Adam Clayton, James Connolly and even one or two players from the Italia '90 soccer team.

bought a VCR device. Cavendish nodded sadly and asked how many other kids had VCRs in their homes. When almost half the class put their hands up, he sighed and said 'not many real families left'. Another time, a boy had written 'Liverpool FC' on his schoolbag and Cavendish brought him in front of the class and asked him why he hadn't written his own parish club's name there instead.

The Irish language was never an end in itself for men like him; it was a talisman to protect us from modernity, technology, liberalism and change.

─╫╫╳─ Shalloween and Other Traditions ─╫╫╳─

Pléascóg is the Irish word for a banger. A more elegant firework would be **tine ealaíne**, which translates literally as fire art... and **dúlasair** means a dark, smoky flame.*

I loved Halloween throughout my childhood – or Shalloween, as Mr Cavendish liked to call it; he thought it was 'a load of American shite' (this seemed a little hasty given that in the early '80s, Irish Halloween was still quite different from the American version – turnips were still carved instead of pumpkins and 'help the Halloween party' was the expression used instead of 'trick-or-treat'). My brothers and I all have birthdays within a month of each other, and Halloween lands right in the middle of this. In fact, my earliest memory is from when I was nearly three years old; I had a Halloween toffee apple in one hand, my dad's big paw in the other and we were in a lift on the way to see my mam and my brand new baby brother in hospital.

* As well as being the best cat name ever, it's also the title of a poetry collection by Doireann Ní Ghríofa.

Samhain is the Celtic festival taken as the precursor to Halloween and is still a huge event in Ireland – it was never quite as popular in England, given that Guy Fawkes Night was their big bonfire event. Perhaps this dissonance gave additional weight to the belief that Halloween was specifically Irish. It certainly was popular here, but not exclusively so – Halloween traditions were popular in Scotland, Yorkshire and Wales too. This makes claims that the Irish brought Halloween to America harder to prove.†
The popularity of this claim hints at the feeling that this holiday is particularly significant in Ireland, and that's indisputable. The overlap of Halloween and **Samhain** tells of a link between Christianity (Catholicism in particular) and a pagan heritage – a range of traditions and superstitions that link us to a past where nature was not a problem to be solved and the subconscious wasn't smothered in learned guilt.

Many of these traditions and superstitions have left their fingerprints on the Irish language, which we will examine here.

† There's plenty of written accounts of Halloween festivities in New England before the influxes of the 1840s.

The Irish for someone who tells ghost stories is **taibhseoir**. Their stories might include a **conriocht** (a werewolf – literally, wolf-shape) or a **bean sí** (a banshee – literally, a faerie woman) or even **púca na sméar**, the blackberry fairy. **Púca na sméar** is the herald of winter, a spirit who finishes off the last of the harvest. Since you ask, he does so by peeing on it. **Piseánach**, meaning lentils or pulses, shouldn't be mixed up with **piseogach**, meaning witchcraft (unless the witch's brew was particularly high on roughage).

In terms of less well-known entities from Irish history and mythology, a **fiachaire** is a raven watcher. They'd try to predict the future (or even just the weather) by watching ravens and looking cool. A **cingciseach** is someone born during the three days of the Pentecost; such folk were believed to be doomed to kill, be killed, or both. The Irish for banana is **banana** – as opposed to **bánánach**, a supernatural beast who haunts battlefields.

Súmaire (or **súmaire fola**) can mean a bloodsucker or a vampire. A **súmadóir** would be a slow, zombie-like person. **Mua** can mean an apparition, a face in a cloud or a mysterious figure that may or may not be real.

The Irish word **alltán** means a monster. It can also mean a wild man. Another Irish word for monster is **anchúinse**, which may also mean a scoundrel.

The Irish for a slayer is **éachtach**. A watcher would be **feighlí**.

Sochraid means a gang of friends; your 'squad', if you will. In less cheerful circumstances, it may refer to a funeral procession. After the funeral, the **réabóir reilige** might turn up; that's the Irish for a grave robber. In the course of his or her career, a *réabóir reilige* might encounter **ainbhlinn** (which doesn't have a direct English equivalent; it means the froth from the mouth of a decaying corpse) as well as a **cnámharlach** or two. *Cnámharlach* is one of the Irish words for a skeleton, coming from **cnámh**, which means a bone.

Depending on the final circumstances, our *réabóir reilige* might even see a **dícheannach**; this is a headless body, but it may also mean a leaderless person (who may or may not also be headless).

All Soul's Night is one of many traditions around the world promising a moment when the boundaries between the worlds of the living and the dead are briefly open. Another reason that Halloween might feel particularly significant in Ireland is the peculiar obsession with death and funerals here. 'A good funeral is better than a bad wedding' is a wonderfully multi-layered bit of wisdom I was offered by older colleagues when I got engaged, which hints at the social aspect of funerals for those outside the immediate family. A **sochraideach maith** is someone who is a regular attendee at funerals; the practice of politicians attending funerals of people they barely know, to raise their local profile among the attendees, is still widespread in Ireland.

A **tórramh** is a wake; it can also mean a gathering or harvesting.

Wren Day

There is some overlap between Halloween and the **Dreolín** which follows it two months later – another pagan festival (winter solstice) that was appropriated to tie in with a Christian feast day. The wren was the king of all birds in Celtic folklore; the story goes that all the birds of Ireland had a tourney to see who could fly the highest and the wren, being small, hid in the eagle's feathers until it reached its maximum height and then launched just far enough ahead to win. The wren was a trickster and a pagan icon; **dreolín** is taken to be a compound of **draoi** (druid) and **éan** (bird). Wrens were associated with divination and a person schooled in **dreanacht** (wren-lore) could tell from the hopping of a wren the time of a person's death.

The wren, in his capacity as a pagan trickster, grassed Saint Stephen out to the Romans, so St Stephen's Day was deemed a suitable occasion to find one, murder it and parade it around the parish. Nowadays a real bird isn't used, but the **lucht an dreolín** (wren boys) still parade around in their terrifying straw outfits and masks.

Wren Day activities are still popular in the western extremes of Ireland, but have also been preserved in the Dublin neighbourhood of Irishtown. Another festival with a link to a pagan past is Puck Fair, the raucous annual gathering in Killorglan named after **poc**, a young goat. Such a creature would be borrowed from the wilds of Kerry and made king for the duration of the festival. Lovers of Shakespeare will recognize a character from *A Midsummer Night's Dream* here, and will be interested to know that the Irish word **púca** means a mischievous fairy.

In Irish, the word **Cáisc** is used for both Easter and Passover. This came from *pascha* in Latin, as the letter P wasn't used in Irish then. Yom Kippur is **Lá an Leorghnímh** in Irish; the literal meaning, day of atonement, is translated directly in this instance, rather than finding an Irish spelling to match the sound of the words (as is the case with **Cabala**, the Irish for Kabbalah).

Speaking of the letter P, the observance of Lent in Ireland is usually punctuated by St Patrick's Day, when participants are entitled to a day of respite from their abstention. In bygone times, no meat would be eaten during Lent and Catholics would dine mostly on herring for the forty days.*
Hence the line in the old poem, *Mo-Chean Do Theacht, A Scadáin* ('Hail Herring, You've Come!').†

* Meat, including chicken, was forbidden in those pre-Vatican II days. However, the puffin (*éan dearg*) was considered to be part-bird, part-fish and eating it was permitted to anyone who could get their hands on one.

•

† These extracts from the poem and its translation are taken from *An Duanaire – Poems of the Dispossessed* (O'Tuama & Kinsella).

A scadáin sheimhe shúgaigh
A chin chumhdaigh an Charghais
A mhic ghádhaigh mo charad
Liom is fada go dtángais.

Herring, gentle and jovial,
our mainstay in time of Lent,
my friends' favourite son,
it was long until you came.

As you can imagine, people were utterly fed up with herring by Easter, when processions and festivals would be held to mock the welcome-outstaying fish. No such processions exist today; commemorations of the 1916 Rising,‡ scheduled to have a symbolic link to Easter (the resurrection of Ireland), are more likely to be held instead.

Cavendish loved Easter; not the eggs or the bunnies or even the time off work, but he loved the Easter Rising. Saying that the Rising was a failure was like saying that the crucifixion of Jesus was a failure, he liked to say.

‡ The Easter Rising was an attempted revolution in Ireland in 1916. It was not a successful military operation, but it galvanized support for an Irish Republic.

Céasta	crucified
Aoine an Chéasta	Good Friday*
An Faí Chéasta	the passive voice

Fuinneoga daite is Irish for stained-glass windows. **Daite** (in this instance, a grammatical form of **dath**) means coloured or dyed, but can also mean fated. Interestingly, **béaldath** means lipstick (literally, mouth-colour) and **béalchrábhadh** means hypocritical religious faith (literally, mouth-piety).

---

* Personally I think *Aoine an Chéasta* is better than Good Friday; the 'Good' part is harder to explain to a child. I also like the poetic relationship between *céasta* and *cáisc*.

Scoilteach	sharp pain*
Teach Scoile	schoolhouse

These are completely unrelated, I'm sure – unless you ask a **déagóir** (teenager). Isn't it interesting that you can't spell *déagóir* without **éagóir** (unfair)? I was about to find out.

* Not to be confused with *scaoilteach*, meaning loose . . . or a laxative.

SECONDARY SCHOOL
The Descent into Adolescence

Níl cara ag cumha ach cuimhne
Memory is sorrow's only friend

Music and memory are old friends; friends who know each other too well. I'm sure that you've had a Proustian moment* or two when a song triggers a memory that pushes others up out of your subconscious with it. For me, the song 'Don't Cry' by Guns N' Roses takes me right back to Carraroe in 1991, sitting on a stone wall between two fields while a girl, in deepest concentration, gave me a biro tattoo on my right arm. She had a Claddagh ring on each hand, one pointing in, one pointing out.† Her friend and my friend were kissing behind a haystack. The song 'I'm Free' by the Soup Dragons brings to mind the tie-dye t-shirts, oxblood Doc

* Yeah, I know Proust's Proustian moment was triggered by a taste rather than a sound, but the point stands, okay?

•

† The direction a Claddagh ring points indicates whether the bearer is single or spoken for.

Martens, Lee jeans and step haircuts that were the gauche uniform of all the other **déagóirí** at the Gaeltacht discos and **céilís**.

I had been in a low place all year; I was the only boy from my primary school to go to my secondary school, and I wasn't making friends fast enough to replace the ones I was losing. When you're thirteen, it feels like everyone else has everything figured out. There's a scene in *A Portrait of the Artist as a Young Man* when a schoolmate confrontationally asks Stephen Dedalus if he kisses his mother at night. When he says yes, they mock him. When he clarifies that actually he does not, they mock him. These jerks are the 'fellows' that his father has warned him not to 'peach' on. I think this is a very pithy account of boys' schools, and I was on the wrong end of countless such exchanges throughout my first year of secondary school. I absolutely hated it. Everything that I liked about myself the previous year, everything that I enjoyed, was interested in or thought I was good at, was ripped down. I had been the best in my class at art, but suddenly I was surrounded by incredibly talented kids. I had been a good all-rounder, but was now struggling – especially in Irish.

My dad had hated secondary school too; he had been sent to boarding school in Tipperary during the Emergency, and one summer afternoon when he met a school acquaintance in a bar, I overheard them describing a 'pretty bad winter' when three of their classmates died from pneumonia and other winter miseries. What must it have been like in the industrial schools if that's what was happening at nice boarding schools? Dad never gave us the 'when I was your age I had to walk ten miles, barefoot, in the snow' line, which gave these occasional disclosures far more impact. What he did do, however, was reiterate his belief that the solution to every problem was more education, and I was struggling with languages in particular.

Clearly a three-week trip to the West of Ireland was in order.

I had spent most of my childhood summers in Ventry and Dingle, so I had witnessed others participating in the Gaeltacht before; I'd be on my knees on the beach, making Star Wars toys fight each other on a sandcastle, only to be disturbed by a stray volleyball or a stampede of teenagers charging towards the ocean. They threw clothes off as they ran into the water, or they jumped in fully dressed – either way, they didn't care. They drank Lilt and laughed like they were in an ad for Lilt. They wore sunglasses and makeup and leather jackets. They knew how to dance, kiss and smoke cigarettes. When you're nine, fourteen-year-olds seem to be the pinnacle of sophistication. The local aul' lads who my mam would chat to on her way back to the shops would laugh about how every summer, the village turned into Tír na nÓg. It sounded magical and I wondered when I'd be old enough to go to the land of the young. Everything that I, as a thirteen-year-old, felt awkward about was something that those Gaeltacht teenagers had successfully resolved. Becoming one would surely fix me.

My Gaeltacht memories are a Gordian knot, and I cannot separate my surging interest in girls and music with my diminishing interest in Irish. With hindsight, I see more connections between these three threads – sex, music and language – and I think that the anxieties, myths and true pleasures of all three overlap enough so that our understanding of one gives insight into the others.

There are different kinds of love and desire. There are different genres of music and keys to play them in. And there are different languages, and languages within them. Just as misunderstandings in love come from expecting all loves to follow the same rules, and disagreements about music are rarely about whether one sequence of notes is objectively superior to another, misunderstandings about language have a mathematical root: it all begins with a failure to count, to match like for like.

The Irish language isn't the same one thing to the people who care about it, nor is the English language. For some people (particularly in the Gaeltacht), Irish is the language they use when buying sausages at the butcher, arguing with the postman or cursing when they stand on a nail. For some fluent speakers, it is a language intimately connected with certain close relationships but not with others. For others, it is an academic objective, a subject to be conquered to get into university (or the civil service, Gardaí or legal profession until recently). For others, it's a second language with charming turns of phrase, a kind of philological heirloom that they like to take out whenever they get a chance. And there are some who like it, but aren't confident enough to use it and have resigned themselves to using it for decorative purposes only. These multiple facets aren't the same as the multiple facets of English and expecting them to match will not lead to satisfactory conclusions.

Written Irish is hard; consider a word like **neamhbhalbh**. A person with no previous contact with the language could be forgiven for thinking this was a typing error, if

not a product of the same chimps-with-typewriters experi-
ment that produced Chumbawamba. Someone fleetingly
acquainted with Irish (from eleven years old in school, for
example) might identify two consonant pairs – **mh** and **bh** –
that both make a 'v' sound. Why do we need two pairs of
letters to make the same sound, especially when we took
the trouble to introduce the letter v to the Irish alphabet?*

A person with a little bit more Irish might look at **neamhbhalbh** and identify two separate words – **neamh** (not or
un-) and **balbh** (mute). Truly, our word for outspoken is a
masterpiece in West-of-Ireland understatement.

Of course, in the old alphabet, each of those **h**'s would've
been a **ponc séimhithe** instead.† If the word had been spelt
phonetically‡ as '*nayvolve*', the letters wouldn't give the
reader any clue to the construction and meaning of the
word, or any indication of how the spelling would change
if it were in a different case.

Some languages have words whose endings change
depending on the position in the sentence. Others have a
beginning that changes. Irish has both.

---

* Unlike Irish, Manx decided to go with phonetic spellings;
while there are lots of other variable factors at play, it
doesn't seem to have led to higher use of that language.

•

† A *ponc séimhithe* is a little dot above a consonant.

•

‡ Spelling phonetically with a PH and a double L is one of
the English language's meanest pranks, along with the S in
lisp and the overall spelling of dyslexia.

However, spoken Irish – what I had been sent to the Gaeltacht to immerse myself in – can be hard too, and matching a word that you've heard to a word you've seen written down can feel like an epic journey. For example, I remember being stopped in my tracks one summer evening in Carraroe by a young woman singing, unaccompanied, a traditional love song mourning a lover who was leaving for America never to return (a **beochaoineadh** is a lament for someone who has not died, but has gone away, presumably forever). When she finished, to much applause, I overheard someone describe it as an **amhrán farraigeach**. This description blew me away almost as much as the performance: **farraigeach**, a seafarer, but also angry and passionate like the sea, full of sealike depth... and with bonus points for singing about someone at the other side of the ocean?* I immediately decided it was my favourite word ever in any language.

When relaying this treasure to my friends, I was swiftly contradicted. Clearly the speaker in question had said (or intended to say) **feargach**, which just means angry and nothing else.

I'm not one to take contradiction lying down, even when all the evidence is against me. *Feargach* isn't the only word for angry in Irish (not by half) and it's intimately connected to the word **fearga**, which means manly or virile. It's a very specific kind of aggressive, entitled anger that's different from **spadhrúil** (moody, given to fits of anger or foolishness) or **deargbhuile** (literally, red angry). It's not a word I would have used to describe a song with sealike depths of passion for a lover across the sea with waves of anger crashing down on the

* Remember, in this context, that *barróg* can mean a hug or a crested wave.

socioeconomic system that tore them apart from each
other. Like 'fetch' in *Mean Girls*, I'm still trying to make
farraigeach happen.

However, there's a difference between clever wordplay
and getting something so wrong that it becomes more
exact than the right answer, and that difference is knowing what you're doing.

Áibhéalaí is the Irish word for an exaggerator. It's not a
widely-used word, because Irish people never exaggerate.

Teenagers, however, do exaggerate – about their knowledge of music, about how little they study and how daring
they are, and about how sexually accomplished they are.
For example, that memorable encounter I described earlier
when I got a biro tattoo from an interesting girl; when I told
the other lads I was housesharing with (in **Tig Uí Cheal-
laigh** – the Kelly household) about it, the only point of the
story that resonated with them was that I
hadn't 'gotten the snog' from her.†

† She was seventeen
and I was thirteen.
Cut me some slack.

Injured pride aside, these conversations
about sexual prowess with teenagers
from around the country were a bracing
introduction to the world of regional
slang. To kiss someone properly could be snog (the term
used in then-popular teen magazine *Smash Hits*, sometimes wishfully assigned an etymological link to the Irish
word **snag**), shift, feek or get off. This last one confused the
country lads, who found it counterintuitive; surely you
were getting on? An attractive girl was a **byoor**, according
to the fellows from Limerick and Galway. The origins of
this one were hotly debated – was it from Irish, or even

Shelta?* After all, the male equivalent, feen, clearly came from Irish (although which Irish word it comes from is up for debate – **féin, fiáin** and Fenian each make a fair claim). Was byoor a phoneticization of BR, short for big ride? Or was it a wordplay rhyme on hoor? Was it just a sound that sounded right and stuck?

Even then, my thirst for word trivia could not be easily slaked. The idea that words for intimate or secret things (kissing, stealing, smoking, borrowing) had borders gripped me; these borders were invisible, porous and a truer reflection of community than constituency, council or parish lines.

---

* *Shelta* is the language of the travelling community; sometimes it is called *cant* (like *caint* – talk or speech – in Irish). While it bears some similarities to Irish, English and Scots, the differences extend beyond what would generally be considered dialect. Like *Verlan* slang in French, *Shelta* often involves reversing words or syllables to create a new term – *lackeen* for cailín (girl) for example.

Insults, Invective and Constructive Criticism

Being a teenage boy means learning to take a slagging and give one back as you repress your many insecurities and anxieties with a forced swagger. It's an exhausting process, but it does present opportunities for creativity and erudition. Consider some of these Irish words the next time you find yourself in such a situation.

There are many words for fool in Irish, but **abhlóir** is a special type of fool: one who complains constantly and pretends to be intelligent. Yet another Irish word for a fool is **blaoiscéir**. Specifically, it means someone whose head is empty like an old eggshell. Ironically, such a person might also be a **bogán**; that's the name of a spineless person and also means an egg with no shell. A **deargamadán** is an utter fool (literally, a red fool – not red-haired but red of face one who's foolishness is plain to see).

A **banránaí** is someone who grumbles and complains rather than confronting matters directly. Of course, that'd never happen in Ireland.

A **bearránach** is an annoying person, one who infuriates you often without realizing it. If you wish to be more specific, a **socadán** is a person with a pointy nose or an interfering busybody. It's not a widely-used word, because we mind our own beeswax, and yet we have two words for it. A **gobachán** also holds both meanings (pointy-nosedness and gossipiness). A spoilsport or killjoy is a **seargánach**.

A **bromaire** is someone who farts a lot, or a self-important boaster. A **smuilceachán** is a sulky person, or a person with an unbecoming nose. A **deiliúsachán** is an impertinent person, such as might be inclined to effrontery and utter cheekiness. **Sciorr** translates as slip, slide or skid; a **sciorrachán** is a pimp.

The Irish word **amhas** can mean boor, hooligan, gangster, caveman, hireling or Tartar. **Amhas beag** is a naughty child. A useless onlooker is called a **gabhgaire**, which translates as go next (the person waiting for their turn). **Scramaire** means a scrounger, loafer, grabber, miser or extortionist.

Corrdhiabhal (literally, an eccentric devil) means

someone who's a little bit odd. Everybody knows one, and they probably also know an **ardcheann** – that translates literally as high head and means someone with notions who ought to be taken down a peg or two. And if you've ever been called a spanner when in Dublin, please note that this comes from **spáinnéar** (a callow youth), not the tool.

The lovely little word **geancach** means snub-nosed. It may also mean rude, surly or having an unpleasant, nasal voice. **Gearrmhuineálach** means short-necked. It can also refer to having an average-sized neck but every other body part is larger than usual. The fine word **lábánach** means a muddy person (literally or figuratively) or a male fish. As an adjective, it means lowbrow.

Geolbhachán means someone with a double chin or heavy, jowly cheeks. **Geadán**, the Irish word for a buttock, can also mean a bare patch on the ground. **Geadánach** means a very unpleasant person.

A **mothaolaí** is a gullible person . . . but do you really want to take my word for it?

Insults and slagging are all great craic, of course, especially when it's the other person's fault for not being able to take it. But sometimes it can get very tiring. The Irish word **aonarán** means someone who is quite happy to be left on their own, as opposed to a **deoraí**, who'd appreciate some company.

Struggling at school is in itself a problem, but I was faced with another; how do you learn a language if you're too shy to talk to anyone? All through primary school I was a chirpy, maybe even over-confident lad who loved chatting away to grown-ups about a wide range of topics. But the

These Irish words sound a bit rude, but are actually grand:

Pionós	penalty
Anall	hither
Arsa	said
Geá	bargepole
Bumaireacht	bragging
Cunta	count
Focal	word
Tit	fall
Scrúdarsa	small particles of butter in buttermilk

sprouting of hair and dropping of testicles had turned me into a socially awkward monster, clumsy as half a horse and as sensitive as a paper cut. Every social interaction was an opportunity for me to make an absolute fool out of myself. A part of me tried to deal with it by enjoying it, by playing the clown, but that never ended well.

The only thing for it was to lock myself in my room and listen to music. I had painted the walls black when I was thirteen; when I returned from the Gaeltacht my mam had repainted them sunflower-yellow.

NÍ THUIGIM
(I Don't Understand)

I've decided to list some linguistic banana skins and potential pitfalls in this section: words that sound a bit similar to unrelated English words, words which can be mistaken for each other when said aloud, and words which surely must involve intentional double meanings, whose roots have been lost in the mists of time. I'll leave it for you to decide which are which.

The Irish for colour-blind is **dathdhall**. While some people are indeed colour-blind, others are just a bit subjective when it comes to describing whatever is in front of them – one person's beige is another person's taupe (or, if you like paint catalogues, Irish cream/hen egg/bare brick/pine nut). Such disagreements are a frequent occurrence with colours in translation.

The Irish term for a black man, **fear gorm**, translates literally as blue man. Just to add to the confusion, bluegrass is **gormfhéar**. One of the theories to explain this is that **fear dubh** (literally, black man) was an existing term for the devil in the centuries before Irish speakers had contact with black people, and **gorm** was offered as a compromise. An Orangeman is **Fear Buí** – literally, a yellow man.

Fionnghlas (the colour of the sea during a storm) is taken as meaning clear green, but **fionn** can also mean fair, blonde or alight. Of course, *fionnghlas* could also refer to the *fionn* (white) of the froth and the **glas** (green) of the water.

As well as meaning green, *glas* has the privilege of meaning grey in some circumstances; blame (or thank) differences between Connemara Irish and the other dialects for that. A grey squirrel, for example, is **iora glas**.* One explanation for this is that *glas* is actually an umbrella term for the spectrum of natural colours between true green (**uaine**) and true blue (*gorm*), which gives a fairer account of the actual fur tones of a squirrel.

* Not to be confused with the celebrated Chicago public radio broadcaster, Ira Glass.

Dearg is the generic term for red. However, as a general rule, living things are **rua** instead of *dearg* – hair, fur, vegetation... even beers. The place name Tonroe in Galway comes from **An Tóin Rua**, which means the red bum. The exception here is plankton, which is **beatha dearg** – red life. Obviously plankton doesn't have the luxuriant hair or foliage to earn the adjective *rua*.†

‖‖‖ ‖‖ ‖ ‖‖‖ ‖‖ ‖ ‖‖‖ ‖‖ ‖ ‖‖‖ ‖‖ ‖

Anduine means an awful and cruel person – not to be confused with **an duine**, which means the person.

‖ ‖‖ ‖‖‖ ‖ ‖‖ ‖‖‖ ‖ ‖‖ ‖‖‖ ‖ ‖‖ ‖‖‖

Bafflingly, one of the Irish names for a puffin is **éan dearg** (literally, red bird) – presumably the red refers to the beak in this instance. There is a third, fancier word for red – **flann** – which precisely means blood red. **Flanshúileach** (literally, blood-eyed) is so much more dramatic than **deargshúileach** or even **sreangshúileach**. Another word for blood red is **cródhearg** – literally, heart red.

How could anyone not adore the lovely word for pink? **Bándearg** (literally, white red) is both pretty *and* sensible. Other compound molecules to describe colours include **flannbhuí** (orange, red-yellow) and **liathchorcra** (lilac, grey-purple).

One final note of colour confusion; green is the colour generally associated with Ireland, but the official colour of the Republic of Ireland is navy; this is the colour of the carpets in Leinster House‡ and on the cover of the constitution.

† Also, an archenemy is *deargnamhaid* – red enemy. Very Cold War.

‡ Leinster House is the location of the Irish Parliament.

Ceilteach means a Celt and **duine ceilteach** means a secretive person. Well, you try getting a straight answer out of one.

Although it may be a source of slight embarrassment in diplomatic circles, **Francach** means a French person and *francach* means a rat. To further complicate matters in Iveagh House,§ the Irish for syphilis is **an bolgach fhrancach** – literally, the French pox.

Interestingly, a hazelnut is **cnó Gaelach** (literally Irish nut)* and **cnó gallda/**

§ Iveagh House is the location of the Department of Foreign Affairs.

cnó Francach (literally foreign nut/French nut) is a walnut. So there. I'm not sure if someone felt that walnuts deserved to be lumped in with rats and syphilis for some reason, but let's extend the spirit of *fraternité* to our nearest neighbouring republic and assume that it's all just a big coincidence.

Yet another meaning that changes on the whim of a capital letter is **Cláiríneach**, a native of Clare, versus **cláiríneach** (a cripple, deformed person), to use the dated language of the Ó Dónaill dictionary. I suspect that this has more to do with two unique words emerging from a shared root (Clare, **An Chláir**, is a flat county, and a person with an injury or disability may be **cionn clár** – laid out) rather than a comment on the folk of the Banner county. Another county that has run afoul of linguistic confusion is **An Mhí**, or Meath; the Irish word **meath** means weakness, decadence, decline or failure.

* Another name for hazelnut is *faoisceog*, which means wee shell. *Faoisce* can mean shell or mollusc.

While **scilling** is the Irish word for a shilling, **scilling Albanach** – literally, a Scottish shilling – is slang for a penny. (If you wish to avoid ridicule and ostracization, remember that the Irish for Scottish is **Albanach**, but Albanian is **Albáinis**.)

Misunderstandings are especially dangerous in the world of politics and economics, where precision and clarity are urgent and important for the right decisions to be made. For example, once they were the same, but now you'd be hard-pressed to mistake **geilleagar na tíre** (national economy) for **geilleagar tíogair** (tiger economy). We live in hope.

The Irish word for an extremist is **antoisceach** – not to be confused with **an Taoiseach**, the prime minister of the Republic of Ireland. Please also be mindful that the Irish for tax is **cáin** and should not be confused with **caoin** (to keen or lament). Contrary to what you may have heard, NAMA† isn't 'enemy' in Irish. The misunderstanding may have come from the **nama** entry in *Dinneen*; **namhaid** is Irish for enemy.

We don't use the term rack-rent (rents that are close or equal to the annual value of a property) much in English anymore; does that mean that rack-renting isn't still a problem, or that it's become so common that it no longer warrants comment? The Irish equivalent of rack-rent is **ainchíos**, which has superficial and coincidental similarities to the word **ainchríost** (antichrist) that do not warrant deeper consideration.

† The National Asset Management Agency (NAMA) is an organization created by the Irish government to deal with the consequences of the 2008 financial crisis.

Tónach means big-bottomed; don't mix it up with **Platónach**, meaning Platonic (unless that's the true Platonic ideal). Speaking of the Greeks, **Gréagach** is Irish for Greek, and can also mean gaudy or flashy. On the other hand, **greaghach** means abounding in horses. Moving in a homeward direction through our bailout brethren, the Irish word **gamba** means a lump or a dollop (**gamba ime** is a dollop of butter). It has nothing to do with prawn tapas. The Irish for prawn is **cloicheán**, not to be confused with **cloichreán**, which means low, murmuring talk – which takes us back to parliamentary proceedings. As well as being the name for the Irish Parliament, **dáil** once also referred to the (sometimes hostile) gathering of

Literally...

Bun na spéire	Skyline	bottom (or base) of the sky
Bréagfholt	Wig	false hair
Gan bhuairt	Nonchalant	without vexation
Macleabhar	Copy of a book	son of [a] book
Dubhshnámh	Diving	black-swimming
Meán Fómhair	September	middle autumn
Bolgchainteoir	Ventriloquist	belly talker
Le crónú le hoíche	Nightfall	tanning/darkening of night
Bléinbheart	Codpiece	groin bundle
Tírín lofa	Banana republic	a rotten little country
Bonnsmideadh*	Foundation	base makeup
Briosca caiscíneach	Digestive biscuit	wholemeal biscuit
Flichshneachta	Sleet	wet snow

* *Bonn* can also mean a medal.

interested parties to a matchmaking. The word **dáileamh** means server or cup-bearer.

An innocent bystander might confuse **gáire** (laugh) with **ga aoire** (the sting of satire). Of course, the target of either could be the same.

NÍ THUIGIM II

Irish Twins

The Irish word for a translator, **aistritheoir**, may also mean a remover (of furniture and other cumbersome things). Both perilous activities.

The phrase 'Irish twins' is used to refer to two children in a family born within a year of each other (although some purists continue to insist that it only refers to children born in the same calendar year). Another possible meaning for this phrase came to me while researching @theirishfor – Irish words with two or more different meanings in English, ideally with a poetic overlap. While such words can be a challenge for new speakers, they have a deep capacity for wordplay that cannot be disregarded. For example, **rún**. This must be one of Irish's most poetic words; as well as meaning a resolution,* *rún* can mean a mystery, a secret, a love or a secret love.

* A new year's resolution is *rún na bliana úire*.

Another is the Irish word for bad influence, **drochanáil**, which can also mean bad breath. **Rí** can mean a monarch or a forearm.

The Irish for nostril, **polláire**, can also mean buttonhole. **Bileog** is one of the Irish words for a leaf; **bileog shúile** is an eyepatch. Another word for leaf is **duille**, which also means eyelid. Speaking of eyes, **gealacán** can refer to the white part of an eye (**gealacán súile**) or the white part of an egg (**gealacán uibhe**). Context is everything.

Uilleann pipes get their name from **uillinn**, the Irish word for elbow. *Uillinn* also means angle; **dronuillinn** is a right angle. Another musical Irish twin is **ceolán**, which can mean a little bell... or a shrieking child (or an adult crybaby).

Méara, the Irish word for mayor, can also mean fingers.

One of the Irish words for low-fat (or light) is **éadrom**. An **éadroman** is a balloon, an air-filled vessel or someone who's a bit of a flake.

Confusingly, the Irish word **scigaithris** can mean either parody or burlesque.

The Irish for unbecoming is **neamhdheas**, which translates literally as non-nice. As a prefix, **neamh** means un- or non-, but as a noun it means heaven. The problem of having contradictory meanings is shared by **tuath**, which means a people or tribe, but can mean rural, sinister or evil when used as a prefix. A **tuathghríosóir** (evil inciter of people) is a sinister demagogue. Speaking of sinister demagogues, the intriguing word **púir** can mean a loss, tragedy or cause of sorrow... or a swarm or crowd. As it can also mean a smoke duct or a stream of smoke, I wonder if it's related to the old Greek word for flame, **pur**?

A bagman in Irish is **málaeir**. This also means a glutton.

Friofac can mean personal restraint... or the barb of a fish hook.

The Irish for superhero is **sárlaoch**. As well as being a prefix for super, **sár** can mean a czar... or bitterness. **Lorg a láimhe** means (someone's) handwriting. **Lorg na súghóg** means the mark or trail left by tears.

Súlach can mean dirty water, sap, dishwasher, manure, discharge, farmyard waste... or gravy.

One Irish term for chatting someone up is **cluain cainte**. **Cluain** can mean persuasion, deception... or a meadow.

Here's one for any conspiracy theorists who think that news outlets are in thrall to some powerful figures in the background: the Irish verb **clóigh** can mean to print... or to tame.

The versatile word **liam** can mean a grumpy, mono-browed singer or a protective father with a specific set of skills.

The Irish word **lúibín** can mean a loop, a buttonhole, a ringlet of hair or a bracket (**idir lúibíní** means in brackets). A leash is **iall**, which can also be a lace, string or line formation; a flight of angels would be **iall aingeal**.

The Irish word **éiric** can mean revenge, retribution, ransom or the satisfaction received for a wrong – paying the eric fine.

As well as meaning forest or woodland, **coill** can mean castrate. Kingswood in west Dublin is **Coill an Rí** in Irish; the king had better watch out!.

Gligín can mean a wee bell, a rattle or noisy thing, or a person whose head contents are as sparse as a rattle.

As well as being the Irish word for a narrator, **reacaire** can mean bait thrown over water to attract fish. The connection here might be the fact that this fishing technique is sometimes called broadcasting.

Comhbhá can mean close friendship, alliance, fellow-feeling... but also rivalry or contention.

Fáil is sometimes translated as destiny (especially in the case of the political party **Fianna Fáil**), but may also mean available (for coalition, presumably).

The Irish for a wooden spoon is **cnáiscín**, which may also refer, figuratively, to a disciplinary threat.

Scailéathan is another word for an exaggerator in Irish. It may also refer to a rush of excitement that may lead someone to exaggerate.

One Irish word for heartthrob is **staic**, which may also mean a big stake. Another is **stail**, which may also mean stallion.

The Irish word **cnábaire** means a hemp-beater, but may also refer to someone who is tall and stooped.

As well as meaning a penny, the Irish word **pingin** can also mean a sheep's second stomach.

Fuinneamh means vigour, momentum or pep. **Fuinneamh a chur i gcroiméal** means to twirl a moustache.

Biorach means sharp or pointy. It may also mean an alert, clever person or the winning card in a game.

Ag stalcadh can refer to the setting of jelly (**glóthach ag stalcadh**) or the stiffening of a corpse (**corp ag stalcadh**).

Goradh generally refers to heating; it can also refer to firing metal, incubating/hatching eggs or even blushing.

A Fada Can Make All the Difference

Steamar	insignificant thing (iota, smidgen, tittle)
Steámar	smug vanity . . . or stale urine
Scal	flash/burst of light
Scál	hot tea . . . or a hero
Cainteoir	talker
Cáinteoir	fault finder (in my family, the Venn diagram of these is a circle)
Staraí	historian/storyteller
Stáraí	a cheeky-peeky starer (or a rude person)
Obó	an exclamation of self-pity
Óbó	oboe (often used in TV when a pitiable character is at large)
Gainneach	scaly
Gáinneach	reedy
Gaire	nearness/proximity
Gáire	laugh
Eitil	to fly/flutter, or flicker as a flame
Éitil	strength or vigour
Gal	valour, fury, warlike ardour
Gál	gall (in plants)

SECONDARY SCHOOL
CONTINUED...
Peig and the *Modh Coinníollach*

The last day of the Gaeltacht was (in the early 1990s anyway) marked by kids tearfully exchanging maudlin messages in the back of each other's copybooks, exchanging addresses and promising to stay in touch. There'd be an intense, emotionally-charged **céilí** that evening where someone would try and organize a midnight swim (or similarly unwise event) which would be too poorly organized to ever materialize. There'd be mayhem the next day on the train back to Heuston Station, as some of the bold kids would reveal that they had purchased alcohol in Galway and would invite us to have our first taste. I had taken the pledge at my Confirmation, and as I took my first sip of Stag lager to the cheers of peers, a voice in my head told me that I was definitely going to hell.

This prediction wasn't far off, as it happened, as I was returning to school.

Every subject in the Leaving Cert curriculum has its bad neighbourhoods. We groaned through English class at W. B. Yeats's inability to take rejection; we struggled to find a way to make calculus and matrices relevant to our own lives in maths; and we felt a thirst as we memorized the molecular formula for alcohol in chemistry. There were two such bad neighbourhoods on the Irish course, ones that are cited frequently when people account for their uncoupling from the language.

In 1995, I started fifth year, the beginning of the Leaving Cert* cycle. This was the same year that two seemingly unrelated things happened. Alanis Morissette released a song called 'Ironic' and Peig Sayer's memoir *Peig* was no longer a required text in Leaving Cert Irish – replaced with the far more crowd-pleasing *A Thig Na Tit Orm*.

I'm sure you're wondering where the hell I'm going with this.

The '90s heralded a horde of articulate, assertive female singer-songwriters – PJ Harvey, Tori Amos, Liz Phair, Fiona Apple, Aimee Mann – but it was Morissette's *Jagged Little Pill* that topped the charts and conquered radio playlists. This success brought her huge attention, which led to a level of scrutiny of her lyrics that she may not have been expecting. Stand-up comedians built whole routines around their parsing of the lyrics from 'Ironic', a song about sadness and disappointment that lists examples of bad things happening. Many of the things listed are indeed ironic (a man afraid of flying,

* The Leaving Certificate (often shortened to the Leaving) is Ireland's end-of-school examination, similar to the A Levels in the UK.

dying in the first flight he ever takes), but many are not (rain on your wedding day, for example). British commentators in particular took great pleasure in using the song as an example of how dumb Americans† don't understand irony, and this lasted for years.

Most people hear a popular pop song more often than they want to, and it's not unusual for lyrics to grate. But Morissette's single came shortly after Snoop Doggy Dogg's breakthrough *Doggystyle*, an album with frequent violent and misogynistic lyrics, and the Beastie Boys hit 'Sabotage', a great song whose lyrics are patently meaningless. However, neither of these acts received the persistent ridicule that greeted the lyrics of 'Ironic'. In fact, anyone criticizing the lyrics of 'Sabotage' would be promptly told to lighten up and anyone criticizing the lyrics to various Snoop tracks would be advised that the artist was using a narrative persona, in keeping with accepted hip-hop tropes, and that the unreliable narrator was an American literary tradition dating back to Huckleberry Finn.‡

The point is that the lyrics of 'Ironic' may not have been the worst of 1995, but they were suited to the kind of critical analysis that was popular and easy; she was successful and subject to a higher standard, she was trying to be clever and had fallen short, her shortcomings supported an existing perception (North Americans not understanding irony), but most of all she was a woman who had gotten a bit uppity and needed to be put back in her box. Once it had

† Ms Morissette is, of course, from Canada. According to her critics, this means she should know better.

‡ For the record (no pun intended), I am a fan of all three artists in question.

been decreed that she had failed in her understanding of irony, people who were insecure about their own grasp of the concept – and there were many – could mock her to reassure themselves that they were right. She wasn't entitled to the lighten up defence or the unreliable narrator defence, apparently.

A similar perfect storm of confirmation bias, schadenfreude and selective critical theory befell *Peig*. It's especially ironic that Peig Sayers wasn't allowed the unreliable narrator defence herself, given how little control she had over the end product. Sayers herself was illiterate, but had acquired a reputation as a great storyteller in a part of the world with many great storytellers. Anyone who has even grabbed a pint with a Kerry woman knows fine well the symphony of sarcasm, droll understatement, wordplay, deft characterization and non sequitur that marks storytellers from this county.

So how did she become this lightning rod for so much hatred and criticism?

Peig Sayers led a simple, private life. She was born in Ventry, had little formal education, went to work as a maid, narrowly missed out on an opportunity to go to America and instead married a fisherman from the Blasket Islands. She never sought fame or stuck her head above the parapet. However, while she was trudging through her many hardships, Blasket life was being observed from afar and decided (by people who didn't live there) to be both a paragon of rural values (by the hard right) and a role model for resisting the savageries of capitalism (by the hard left). Postcolonial societies need to reject the recent past and replace those ideas with something authentic and honourable, and the Blaskets had it. These were values that needed to be instilled in everyone through the education system.*

However, the low literacy rate on the islands and the wider Gaeltacht meant that there wasn't a body of literature describing this life. Enter Peig's son, Maidhc, who took dictation of her life story as well as her retelling of Kerry folklore. It's unlikely that Peig knew how severely her own work was going to be bowdlerized, even if she was self-editing her stories to spare her son's blushes. But Peig – a female storyteller from an era when women rarely had their voices heard – didn't stand a chance against brand Peig ©.

Stories are just stories – they have beginnings, middles and ends, goodies and baddies, conflicts to be resolved and maybe even a subplot. But sometimes stories aren't just stories. Much as John Boy's memories of Walton Mountain in the Depression were consciously presented in the '70s as an antidote to Watergate, Vietnam, hippies, dope fiends and feminists, Peig's stories were packaged and presented not purely on their own merits but as an antidote to modernity.

* Certainly, they were preferable in the eyes of policymakers to the 'values' presented in the existing canon of subversive and erotic Irish-language poetry.

Peig has proven to be popular with adult learners who have chosen to study Irish voluntarily and readers of Peter Carey's Booker-winning *True History of the Kelly Gang* will recognize a folk tale in that book which is a retelling of a story from Peig's repertoire; it concerns a man who makes a deal with the devil and proceeds to use ingenious loopholes to postpone handing over his soul. Peig's reputation has run afoul of a similar Faustian trade.

YOU REMIND ME
OF SOMEONE

A s well as attending the Gaeltacht, I was lucky enough
to go on a French exchange as a teenager. I stayed
with a French family for a few weeks one summer, and
then their son stayed with us. While my hosts were based
just outside St Étienne (the hub of the French arms industry), they took me with them to visit Saint-Tropez. I had
never seen such opulence before in my life; the newspaper
I took with me on the flight over had an article that cited
owning a second television as evidence of a family having
'more money than sense'. But Saint-Tropez had yachts and
sports cars and beautiful people in beautiful clothes. As I
admired the yachts from the shore and wondered what I'd
call my own, I saw one with the name *Saoirse* (freedom). A
few minutes later I saw another with the name Tír na nÓg
(land of eternal youth). I pointed these Irish names out to
the host family. The *grandpère* smiled, and later took me on
a drive where he showed me some mansions on the Côte

d'Azur that had Irish names too; *Ard Rí* (high king) was one that I still remember.

Upon my return to Ireland I told my family and friends about the Irish people who had 'done good' and ended up in the South of France. Not everybody was happy for them.

'Fuckers.'

'Thieves.'

'Probably born with most of it.'

'Nothing that actually needs to be done ever pays that well.'

Perhaps, I said, but isn't it impressive that they chose to name the symbols of their success in Irish? Again, some grumblings.

'There's no way of measuring the number of Irish people who've named their mansion in English or French based on your "scientific research methodology", Darach.'

'I'm sure that's *exactly* why Jimmy Connolly* kept fighting after taking a bullet in the leg in 1916; so fuckers could name their yachts in Irish and live in tax havens.'

And then the dropkick goal:

'Yeah, they found one Irish word that they like. Big wow – I don't see anyone putting the *Modh Coinníollach* of a verb on the side of their yacht or on the front of their mansion.'

It is delightful, another friend added, that there are so many charming words and even phrases in the Irish language, but when it came to the business of entire sentences, then there was no avoiding the unlovely mechanics of Irish grammar. Wasn't it 'a bit Irish' that *Gaeilge* pilfers

* James Connolly, Glasgow-born founder of the Irish Labour Party, union activist and revolutionary. Connolly was the leader of the Irish Citizen Army in the 1916 Rising, which led to his execution.

so many ugly words from English but refrains from borrowing that language's grammatical forms?

When I, as a teenager, complained about the difficul-
ties of the *Modh Coinníollach* to my dad, he said that its
difficulty was the whole point – the MC is a grammatical
form for whingers, moaners and procrastinators. It is used
for making excuses. But the true spirit of Ireland burned
like a flame in the language itself; *Gaeilge* wanted you to
live simply and honourably, to not make excuses and to
commit unconditionally. Once the oppressor made us
speak English, he made it too easy to make excuses and
the country was ruined.

A little tongue-in-cheek, perhaps.

The Irish conditional tense has developed a bit of a reputation for being frustrating – when I was studying tax years
later, I remember a lecturer telling us that 'VAT on property is the *Modh Coinníollach* of the Irish tax system' – even
though it compares favourably to the conditional tenses of
other languages. Every subject in school has its bogeyman
topic, and in languages it's usually advanced grammar.
Once you have a tense that doesn't have a ghost named
after it in *A Christmas Carol*, people
lose interest. Future perfect? Pluper-
fect? Away with ya. The more abstract
grammatical forms are victims of what
I call the spiral stairway problem; you
know exactly what a spiral stairway
is, but if you are asked to describe
it without using your hands (or the
words spiral or stairway) you either
get tongue-tied or resort to extremely
obscure terminology.†

† After years of using
the spiral stairway
example to explain
this phenomenon, I've
settled on 'an inter-
storey passageway
where the sequence of
steps rotates around a
central axis'.

We don't think about the grammatical rules of our own language much – whether a verb is irregular or not rarely (in other words, never) even occurs to us in speech. Untangling ourselves from native irregularity and embracing a new irregularity is so frustrating that we rarely stop to ask which language is objectively less fucked up.

Universally, conditional tenses have three moving verb parts:

If	**I had graduated**	from college,	**I would have**	**become** a lawyer.
If	**I were**	single,	**I would**	**ask** her out.
If	**I win**	the lottery,	**I will**	**quit** my job.

To English speakers, this all looks pretty handy – the first part (the false past) is a baby sentence with an 'if' stuck front of it, the second part has two verbs. An Anglophone, however, would not consider the annoyances of the irregular verb 'would' for non-native speakers – it's an irregular verb for starters, it has a stupid silent 'l', and what's the bleedin' point of having it *and* the 'if' at the start of the sentence? Queen's English Anglophones snigger at *ain't no* and the French double negative, but they carry around their double conditional with pride.

Humour me for a second and imagine if English had an arrangement like the following:

If	I had graduated	from college,	I become	a lawyer.
If	I were	single,	I ask	her out.
If	I win	the lottery,	I quit	my job.

This is the skeleton of the conditional mood in Irish – it applies to the verbs in the 'false past' part of the sentence and the 'excuse' part of the sentence, two verbs instead of three.

For a struggling student of Irish trying to translate a conditional English sentence one word at a time, the MC is a disaster. But for a multilingual university graduate, comparing Irish to other languages and considering the possibility of translating sentences with multiple conditions, it has a cleanliness to it.

However, this is what people talk about when they talk about travel (and the study of languages) broadening one's mind. It makes you notice the invisible assumptions you've been carrying around.

_Y_ You Remind Me of Someone... _Y_

The Irish for autocorrect is **uathcheartaigh**. This well-intended feature often feels like it does more harm than good, and anyone with a smartphone will have sent (and received) a bafflingly worded text that can only be explained by the electronic replacement of an intended word with an unintended one. This can cause untold havoc.

The laws of mathematics and probability mean that with twenty-six letters in the Roman alphabet and a high incidence of vowels, occasionally a spelling form is going to exist in two different languages with alternative meanings. This can be especially confusing when one language has a lot of loanwords from another (as Irish does from English). I've listed some here, including some that aren't exact matches but look tantalizingly close:

Fear means man and **bean** means woman; **eagla** means fear and **pónaire** means bean.

Smut in Irish means a stump or sulky expression. The term for talking smut is **ag gáirsiúlacht**.

A Fada Can Make All the Difference

Geis	taboo
Géis	scream
Saith	bad/evil
Sáith	a (decent sized) meal
Maiteach	forgiving
Maíteach	begrudging
Brach	yellow gunk in the corner of eyes after sleep
Brách	eternal (go brách means forever)
Brath	perception/spying/betrayal
Bráth	doomsday
Sléachtadh	genuflection
Sleachtadh	havoc/destruction
Neimhe	heaven (gen. of neamh)
Néimhe	brightness (gen. of niamh)
Iolach	a howl (of victory/exultation)
Íolach	pagan

The Irish for bee is **beach** (but in Irish, the ch is pronounced like Christmas: *bay-ach*). The Irish for beach is **trá**.

The Irish for atheist is **aindiachaí**, as opposed to **athéist**, which means to rehear something.

Bruscar means rubbish, not busker. The Irish for busker is **fán-aisteoir**, which translates literally as wandering player.

So-lasta means flammable or excitable. It doesn't mean so last year/week/season. (So last year would be **chomh anuraidh**.)

Ríora means a royal dynasty, as opposed to **rí-rá**, which means commotion, hullabaloo or a nightclub on Dame Court.

Seafóid doesn't mean seafood, it means nonsense. The Irish for seafood is **bia na mara**.

Gréasaí doesn't mean greasy, it means shoemaker. The Irish for greasy is **bealaithe**.

The Irish for the sea is **farraige** – not to be confused with Farage, something that should get back in the sea.

LOST WORDS

Awhile back (around 2013) a British newspaper requested suggestions from its readers on their least favourite new words, especially Americanisms. Readers were only too eager to nominate suitably irritating terms, but two points became apparent upon closer inspection: many of the new words weren't new, and many of the Americanisms weren't American. In fact, Winston Churchill himself had used OMG in a letter in the '40s. Encouraged by this – and probably delighted to defend American English after such a slur – the good people over at *Slate.com* responded by examining the movement of loanwords since the dawn of the Internet, and found that, contrary to popular belief, it was American English that was being invaded in the twenty-first century – the growing popularity of soccer, the dominance of Harry Potter on the bookshelves and the fact that American journalists frequently used the *Guardian* website as a research source for international stories meant that terms like minger, ginger, university, autumn and wanker were trickling into the United States' vernacular.

This epiphany replaced a visible but non-existing quandary with an existing, no-longer-invisible one: why are Americanisms in British English assumed to be so bad, and should Britishisms in American English be seen as a good thing, a bad thing or just a thing?

American English is one of the wonders of the modern world. In the early nineteenth century, the United States was not unlike the modern European Union with its plurality of languages. Relations with Britain were terrible following the Revolution and subsequent conflicts. The Louisiana Purchase and a massive influx of German immigrants meant that there were other, more obviously attractive candidates than English for the lingua franca of this young country; Thomas Jefferson in particular thought that English was the least attractive of a suite of options for the new republic. In fact, Hebrew or Greek were suggested as politically neutral options that would mean no one group would lose out to another. Greek, Latin and Hebrew town names (Annapolis, Syracuse, [Jeru]Salem) still litter the East Coast as a souvenir of this time, as well as America's two main political parties – *democrat* and *republican* are Latin and Greek words for the same thing, the rule of the people. Merriam and Webster had their work cut out for them as they sought to advocate a version of English that was familiar to most Americans, but simplified for non-native speakers and sufficiently different from British English to be their own. Although Anglophones scoff at 'color' and 'ax', it's safe to say that the twentieth century would have ended differently if Fifth Avenue in New York had been *Funftestrasse* – which it could have been, if German had become the official language.

Things weren't so straightforward for English in the

United Kingdom either. The nineteenth century was an age of discovery and invention, but scientists in Britain weren't naming their discoveries (like dinosaurs, elements and new devices) in their native language. This appalled the Dorset poet William Barnes, who thought that naming a new invention photograph instead of sunprint or light-writing favoured one dead language (ancient Greek) over another (Anglo-Saxon) for no fair reason. His campaigns to replace words of French origin (conscience, politics) with their proper Anglo-Saxon equivalents (inwit, state-craft) did not get very far. These weren't the stylings of a pre-UKIP faction; Barnes saw his activism as a utopian movement. Historically, the English language had a class system beaten into its dictionary – the people rich enough to eat meat referred to it by different words (mutton, beef or pork) than did the farmers who raised it (sheep, cows or pigs). This was exacerbated by the fact that grammatical rules were being forced into English (such as avoiding the split infinitive, or beginning a sentence with 'and') based on the flimsy premise that if a sentence form couldn't exist in Latin, it shouldn't exist in English.

With its silent letters, arbitrary rules and its 'high' and 'low' words for the same thing, English was a language that it was easy to feel excluded from in the nineteenth century. It was in this context (as well as a result of other more well-documented factors like famines, emigration, land wars and so on) that the Gaelic Revival organizations emerged from the 1870s onwards. Sometimes I feel that Irish may have aped some of English's failings at this time rather than learning from them, and the urge to promote a language 'as good as' English may have been confused with the promotion of one as complicated as English.

For people of my dad's generation, born in the first decade of the Free State, the language was a source of pride, a collective mission and a stepping stone towards a new meritocracy – at least for the people lucky enough (or unlucky enough) to stay in Ireland as adults. The fact that English was the vernacular was, of course, someone else's fault... until eventually a point was reached where this was no longer true. While Hebrew was successfully reintroduced in the fledgling state of Israel,* *Gaeilge* had less luck with Irish schoolchildren bred for export, and a language once associated with a cry for freedom became the vocabulary of instruction, permission and punishment.

* There's a forest outside Nazareth named after Éamon de Valera.

Here's a selection of words that have fallen from use and, in some cases, aren't listed in modern Irish dictionaries anymore. Some of them give an insight into a very different world.

──⦚⦚✗── O'Brien's Dictionary, 1768 ──⦚⦚✗──

Dolbh	sorcery
Dolbhad	fiction

Neither of these two words are in modern dictionaries anymore, which is a shame. I think that their meanings are intensified by their similarities to each other. I found them in Bishop O'Brien's dictionary,† which was first published in 1768. As you can imagine, research methods, standard spellings and peer-review systems have improved a lot since the decade Wolfe Tone‡ was born, and this text is now an obscure footnote§ in the history of the language.

† John O'Brien was the Catholic bishop of Cork. During the penal laws, Catholic priests (including O'Brien himself) in Ireland were typically educated in France or Belgium and O'Brien was concerned that a lack of Irish might reduce their ability to conduct pastoral duties. This was the inspiration for his dictionary.

•

‡ Theobald Wolfe Tone, before becoming a leader of the ill-fated 1798 Rebellion in Ireland, was expelled from Trinity College for duelling.

Having said that, a dictionary is a snapshot of a moment in time, and the moment that O'Brien preserved was a fascinating one, just before the 1798 Rebellion and the subsequent events that would change Ireland and Irish forever: the Act of Union, the Famine and mass emigration to the United States. In that context, I think it's worth a look to see what Irish was like before the traumas that came to define it occurred.

The entry for **mal** states that this word can mean a king or prince, a poet, a soldier or champion, or a tribute, tax or subsidy (I love the idea of a soldier-poet called Mal who becomes a king). Similar poetic potential is found

§ Not without cause, to be fair; Bishop O'Brien draws inferences from superficial similarities between the Hebrew and Gaelic languages that don't stand up to scrutiny, and intriguingly refers to the priests of ancient Egypt as druids. Cool idea for a graphic novel; bad idea for an academic text.

in the entry for **deimhe**, meaning both darkness and protection. Opposing the combination of darkness and protection would be **corrchoigilt**, a word without a direct match in English. It means the strange, coloured glow in embers or a person full of mischief.

Dricc angry or a dragon*

Gus death, anger or a desire/inclination

Loitim to hurt or wound. **Loiteóg** is listed as the word for nettles

Tainisteacht O'Brien links the modern word for the deputy prime minister (**Tánaiste**) to the word thane, best known to students of *Macbeth* as a senior vassal

Cua'uinne worm-eaten nuts

Interesting word neighbours from this dictionary include...

Mathardacht the right of a person's mother
Matharorn matricide

Bes the belly... or rent/tribute
Bescna peace... or any land that is inhabited

Eascoman dirty, filthy or nasty
Eascomata satisfied

Liachac hog's dung
Liach a spoon

---

* The Finnish word for a dragon, *lohikäärme*, translates literally as salmon-snake, intruigingly combining two creatures with huge mythological significance in Ireland (the salmon of knowledge and Saint Patrick's nemesis).

Duibhelneach	a necromancer
Duibhgeann	a sword/dagger
Duibhgeinte	'the black nations' – a disused euphemism for the Danes
Duibhiliath	the spleen
Ea'da'illeach	an Italian
Ea'daingean	weak, not strong
Ea'daire	a jealous lover
Eadairmeas	the art of invention

There are some Irish twins in this book too...

Gleódh   a sigh or groan... or cleaning and scouring

Fadhb   a question or enigma, a knot, a mole, a raven or a widow

Meilg   milk... or death

Meas   a weapon, a salmon or a foster child

Tuiridh   a request, an elegy or a pillar

Badhb   'the North, a tract of land, a Royston crow or other ravenous bird, a faerie woman or a quarrelsome woman'

Gall   an Englishman,† a Gaul or a cock

---

† O'Brien states 'According to the modern acceptation [sic] of the word signifies an Englishman; as *sean-ghaill* the old English, or Strongbonians, the Danes or any other foreigners are in Irish writings called *Gaill* . . . but the true meaning of the word is *Galli*, the Gauls, those from ancient Gaul, now called France.'

Some of O'Brien's definitive definitions...

Tarbhan'a   'a parish bull, a bull that is common to the whole district'

Sramh   'a jet of milk gushing forth from a cow's udder'

Tóit   smoke or vapour. **Tóiteamh** means smoky; **toithghiobhair** is a prostitute and **toith-leannan** is a concubine

Ba'rdamhail   'addicted to satires or lampoons'

Gamal   'a fool or stupid person, is the same in letters and sound with Hebrew Gamal, which means a camel, the most stupid of all beasts'

——⸾⸾⸾× —— O'Reilly's Dictionary, 1864 ——⸾⸾⸾×

How come **omhnach** isn't in the **foclóir** anymore? I often need to describe things that are both terrible and frothy. For the sake of coffee, beer and the sea, we need to bring *omhnach* back. The Irish for frothy (but not necessarily terrible) is **sobalach**. Please note that it doesn't share the Australian meaning of frothie (a beer)... yet. And how did we lose as versatile a word as **fuince**, which can mean a fox, a talon or a crow. These are just three of the words included in O'Reilly's dictionary that didn't make the cut for more modern collections. O'Reilly had a talent for definitions that must have influenced Dinneen forty years later; his entry for *ur* is:

'a grave; a fringe, border, brink, limit, bound; evil,
mischief, hurt, wickedness; slaughter; the sun; fire,
flame, hearth; a beginning, a moist place, a valley...
generous, noble-hearted, free'

Similarly, consider this entry for the nice, short word *cró*:

'Death. An iron bar; the eye of a needle; a flock,
a fold; children; might, valour; a hut, hovel, pen,
cottage, fortress'

Cró is not to be confused, of course, with his entry for *cro*,
which he lists as meaning witchcraft. His dictionary has
a large number of entries for sorcery, witchcraft, death,
mystery and evil – many of which have some very seren-
dipitous word neighbours:

Tairfhiodhbhach	Transylvanian[*]
Tairgheabhadh	woe, desolation
Dealánach	lightning
Dealan-Dé	butterfly
Comharsnamhuil	neighbourly
Comart	killing
Upadh	a sorcerer or witch
Upaire	a sorcerer, charm-monger

---

[*] These entries predate the publication of *Dracula* by
about thirty years.

Upóg	a witch, a pretended [sic] druidess
Uptha	sorcery, witchcraft
Digla	evil
Dighle	very pure or immaculate
Ruithim	I run
Rúitín	a child that delights to play in the dirt; the ankle-bone, a fetlock
Ruithleán	a riddle
Dalbh	a lie, contrivance
Dalbha	impudent, forward
Dalbhdha	sorcery
Dalc	fire

Freud suggested that blinding or eye-gouging in dreams or literature were metaphors for castration. I wonder what he'd have made of the word **aidhcleadh** (which means eye-biting) and its absence from modern dictionaries. It's possible that since this word was last seen in the nineteenth century, food has become more plentiful in Ireland and nobody needs to bite anyone else's eyes anymore.

Baisde is listed here as meaning both Baptist and fornicator. Other 'Irish twin' double-meanings include **mallacht** (a curse or modesty), **dáiltín** (a foster child, a jackanapes or a puppy) and **ursanach** (a doorkeeper, bearish, having the qualities of a bear).

Unlike Bishop O'Brien's work, this dictionary was published after the Famine and the devastation that followed.

One impression that was left on the language recorded here is **tamhthaoí** (dead of the plague).

⧗ Dinneen's Dictionary, 1904 and 1926 ⧗

Fiair-bhrígh isn't in the more recent dictionaries; intriguingly, it means perverse skill. It's one of a number of entries in Father Patrick Dinneen's beloved *foclóir*, which is more of a labour of love than your average lexicon. Dinneen was a Jesuit who taught at Clongowes,* before deciding to turn his back on the comforts and satisfactions of teaching and pastoral duties to work on his *foclóir* full time. His combination of Jesuitical academic acrobatics and native-speaker heritage made for a unique alchemy; in particular, his own definitions suggest a poet cursed to be able to share his gift only through the medium of a dictionary.

The frothy water that spreads over the sand as a wave breaks is **borr-uisce** – literally, fancy/proud/plump water. Why did people stop using such a beautiful expression? More urgently, how did **faolshnámh** ever fall out of use? Dinneen translates it as meaning gliding like a wolf (literally, wolf-swimming).

* He would've been there in the 1890s when Joyce was a student, but proving that they ever shared a classroom could be hard – they both left inauspiciously. Either way, Joyce did refer to Dinneen's dictionary in the 'Scylla and Charybdis' chapter of *Ulysses*.

Speaking of our canine and animal friends, **gadhrach** is another regrettably obsolete adjective from Dinneen's dictionary. It means fond of dogs or abounding in dogs. Surely there's still a place for this word in common parlance?

The *recherché* word **piollárdaidhe** means a trespassing

goat, or a person with such qualities. Another animal-human morphing word would be **faingín** (derived from **faing**, a raven), which means a tall, good-for-nothing girl. **Faing dhíomhaoin** is said of a nimble but lazy person – we all know one of those. Intriguingly, Dinneen includes a word, **meanncán**, specifically to describe a market for socks. For those who cannot make it to the *meanncán*, it's good to know that **cosnochta** means barefoot. **Tae cosnochta** (literally, barefoot tea) is tea served without milk or sugar* – the only kind of tea served in Lough Derg, where pilgrims would typically be barefoot.

The extremely useful word **athghnó** is work you do that wasn't done properly the first time.

Although Dinneen left the Jesuits and the elegant surroundings of Clongowes to live like a pauper in pursuit of his white whale, he didn't completely reject the elitism associated with that order;† in particular, he turned his nose up at Dublin-born Irish speakers. One such Irish speaker was Patrick Pearse,‡ who published his first stories using the nom de plume of Colm Ó Conaire, a Connemara **seanchaí**, for fear that his half-English, half-Dublin background might lead to them not being taken seriously. While reviewing these stories, Dinneen found the authenticity of the prose style lacking, comparing it to the way Irish was actually spoken in the Gaeltacht as follows:

'It (actual Gaeltacht Irish) may at times be over-salted and over-dosed with the water of **béarlachas**, but

---

* Or biscuits, presumably...

•

† Not all Jesuits, of course, but even the liberation theology hippy Jesuits cannot deny that the order has an association with elitism.

it is genuine mountain butter all the same and not clever margarine. I am afraid the storyette about the **píobaire** smacks more like the margarine of the slums than pure mountain butter.'

It's pretty ironic that Pearse put so much effort into creating an authentic Gaeltacht persona only to be found out by not having enough *béarlachas*. If Pearse was unhappy with this review, he had the last laugh when the original plates for Dinneen's dictionary were destroyed during the 1916 Rising.

‡ In English, his name was Patrick Pearse, in Irish it was *An Piarsach* – he wasn't on for combining the two forms and wouldn't have appreciated being known as Padraig Pearse.

A new version was finally assembled and published in 1926, which is the one still loved today. Who wouldn't love a dictionary with entries like **uathach** (an ancient female teacher of warriors), **iníon carbaidh** (a chariot daughter; a poetic term for an illegitimate daughter) and **fáiltín** (a male visitor, meddler or interferer)?

✕‖✕‖✕‖✕ Other Lost Words ✕‖✕‖✕‖✕

The following words have been taken from the Royal Irish Academy's *Dictionary of the Irish Language* (DIL for short), which records entries of the old and middle stages of the Irish language. It was published in 1913, preceding modern spelling conventions. As it is a record of older material, it does not capture the mood of Irish in the year it was published, but trawls deeply into the language's troubled subconscious and buried memories.

The DIL is intentionally exhaustive and therefore

includes some entries that only cite a single source; later dictionaries have either deemed these words too fanciful or their sources too unreliable. Philologists have a term, 'ghost words', to describe words that are present in dictionaries but nowhere else. It's fair to say that, while not necessarily ghost words, the following terms might be met with blank stares if you strike up a conversation in a bar in Carraroe or Dunquinn.

I'm not sure how this ever fell out of use, but the lost word **cendail** means the heads of decapitated enemies. Similarly, **bibseach** means to kill (or put someone to death) twice.

Ainces was a legal concept in old Ireland that refers to an act that is not justified, but is made necessary by the pursuit of a justified action. The example given in DIL is that a man may not be entitled to burn down his neighbour's house, but if he is honour-bound to slay his neighbour and there is no other way to achieve this, the burning would be an *ainces*.

The lost word **dallchéim** means a step taken in the dark, literally or figuratively; it's a combination of **dall** (blind) and **céim** (step).

The *recherché* word **cannabhar** doesn't mean cannabis; it means bits of seaweed on a beach. A wholly different weed.

Adharca bruic are badgers' horns – something non-existent or imaginary (like a red herring).

Fuilmain means a toe that is bruised or bloodied (or both) from (presumably unintentional) contact with a wall, door or idiot. It's possible that the toe may have been bloodied after meeting someone who's a bit **armchar** – that old adjective means a fondness for weapons.

A **cumal** was a female slave. If a man got another man's *cumal* pregnant, he was obliged to find a substitute for her.

Ruidles is a combination of someone's idiosyncrasies and their very essence; it means those qualities and details that are unique and distinctive to them.

Ogham

The Irish for an archaeologist is **seandálaí**, not to be confused with **seansálaí**, which means a chancer.

Before we leave lost words, take a moment to consider our lost alphabet. Ogham is the pre-Latin alphabet of the Celts, and was written and read vertically. Most existing ogham writing available to scholars is carved in stone, but it's not unreasonable to assume that it could also have been written on less durable materials that have not lasted the millennia since.

Ogham has held some popularity in the world of tattoo artists and jewellers (John Rocha designed an anti-racism pin in the mid-2000s that was a combination of ogham forms and Chinese lettering). Charmingly, each letter is named for a tree or plant.

ailm	pine	A
beith	birch	B
coll	hazel	C
dair	oak	D
eabhadh	aspen	E
fearn	alder	F

gort	ivy	G
ifín	gooseberry	I
luis	rowan	L
muin	vine	M
nion	ash	N
peith*	dwarf elder	P (later alphabet)
ruis	elder	R
sail	willow	S
tinne	holly	T
uath	whitehorn	H
úr	heath	U

* As you can see from my helpful asterisk, there was no letter P in early ogham. There's an apocryphal tale that de Valera insisted that the letter V be included in the Irish alphabet to accommodate his own name; perhaps Saint Patrick did the same centuries earlier?

Of course not. That would be ridiculous.

FILM

Léirmheastóir is a professional critic [**léir**: clever; **meastóir**: assessor] unlike a **dímheastóir**, who is just a very disparaging person. Of course, a person could be both.

The Irish for a silent film is **balbhscannán**. A title card (or intertitle) used in silent film as a substitute for dialogue is translated as **idirtheideal** in Irish. I have a nerdy interest in silent film, early talkies and the Irish connection: James Joyce opening the first cinema in Ireland, the unlikely production of *Man of Aran* and Hitchcock's early attempt to bring Sean O'Casey to the screen. The silent era came to an end around the same time that the Hays Code* came into effect (1930), so many of these works are more artistically and

* The Motion Picture Production Code (better known as the Hays Code) was the Hollywood studios' code of censorship, enforced by Irish-American Joseph Ignatius Breen. As well as obvious no-nos like sex, nudity and profanity, the code prohibited sympathy for criminals, scenes of childbirth and negative presentations of the leaders of other countries.

thematically daring than the more modern content that followed them. There's an analogy in there somewhere.

A horror film is **scannán uafáis**, unless you're specifically referring to a monster film – that'd be **scannán arrachtaí**. If your Irish horror film screenplay doesn't have a title yet, **marbhsholas** (meaning half-light) translates literally as dead light. Or maybe you'd prefer the charming word **fuilbhreac** (blood-speckled or bloodstained)? The Irish for revenge is **díoltas. Díol** can mean sale or payment; **is é do dhíol é** means 'it serves you right'. Speaking of revenge and payment, the word for purest gold is **deargór**... not to be confused with **deargár**, defined as a carnival of bloodshed.

Foclóir.ie says the Irish for chick flick is **scannán románsúil do mhná**, which seems a little on the nose (literally, romantic film for women). Suggestions I've received that are a bit snappier include **scannán na lachan** (**lacha** being slang for a young woman, as well as meaning a duck) or the portmanteau **scamnán**. Some cinematic terms are direct translations: **scannán gorm** is a blue film, a B movie is s**cannán B** and *film noir* isn't changed at all. Having said that, some thought went into arthouse film (**scannán sainealaíne** – expert or niche film), blockbuster (**scannán mór eachtraíochta** – big adventure film) and my favourite, spaghetti western – **scannán buachaill bó Bolognéise**, a Bolognese cowboy film.

As for technical terms, slow motion can either be **mall-ghluaiseacht** or **slómó**, and CGI is **íomhánna ríomhghinté** (or IR for short). A flashback in a film or TV show is **spléachadh siar** – literally, a backward glance.

OUR WORDS

My friend José is from León in Spain, and is an even bigger film buff than I am. During his seven years living in Ireland, he found that he could no longer watch films dubbed into Spanish – not because of the unrealistic lip movement, but rather because of the artifice of the translation itself. For example, the first *Die Hard* film was called *The Glass Jungle* in Spanish. There's no literal translation for the phrase 'die hard' in Spanish, and someone thought that 'glass jungle' at least conveyed the idea that this was an action film with lots of broken glass. Then came *Die Hard* 2 and 3... and the name started to make even less sense.

Words resist translation for all sorts of reasons, and terms can have a completely different meaning in the context of a sentence – referring to a man as 'Mr O'Reilly' might be normal in a business phone call, overly formal at a social gathering, or a pointed dig at his not having a PhD in a university context. If a set of words as plain as 'Mr O'Reilly' can have so many possible inflections in English, what happens when you translate it into French or German?

There was another thing that bothered José about the Spanish-dubbed Hollywood films of his youth: sometimes a film would have a character speaking Spanish (usually a cleaning lady, a drug dealer or a sultry temptress). When a foreign language is used to convey otherness, how do you present this to the others themselves? Sometimes the translators feel compelled to become editors; for example, when *The Simpsons* is translated into German, little Uder (the exchange student who is from Dusseldorf but dresses in a stereotypically Bavarian outfit) becomes Swiss.

Loanwords in English were also a problem – what's Spanish for *manana* as it is understood by Anglophones?* The impact of many loanwords in English comes from the qualities attributed to their source language – *achtung, debonair, espresso*... and, of course, *craic*.

Here are some words and expressions in Irish that either have no direct equivalent in English, or a very different context to their English equivalent, or that otherwise translate asymmetrically.

Gréinleacha doesn't have an exact match in English; it means grass that a cow has previously shat on and which remains somewhat distressed or imprinted. I know; somewhere a cow is smiling and thinking 'because of me, they have to have a word'. Continuing on this theme, the useful verb **bualtaigh** means to smear something (or someone) with shite. A dried-up cowpat is a **buarán**, and **aoileach** is an Irish word for dung or manure – not to be confused with **aile**, which is a row of sods outside a stack of turf, or aioli, which is a 'notiony' garlic mayonnaise.

* There's an apocryphal tale about George W. Bush mocking France as being so socialist that their language had no word for entrepreneur.

Amárach	tomorrow
Amanathar	the day after tomorrow
Amainiris	the day after the day after tomorrow

A **crapaire** is one who shrinks, condenses or crushes things. It has nothing to do with poo. **Crap leat!** means 'Go away, you!' The related word **crapshúileach** means peering or looking at someone/something with narrowed eyes. It does not mean having crap in one's eyes.

An archaism is **ársaíocht** in Irish; a person whose speech is peppered with archaisms (talking out of their arse, perhaps?) would be **ag caint ársa**.

Fíoch may mean a feud or anger/fury. It may also refer to a village or townland, a place where a feud might occur. Interestingly, **fíocas** means haemorrhoids. Such feuds often have their beginnings in disputed wills. **Iaró** is one of the words in Irish for a descendant. Completely unrelated, I'm sure, to **iaróg**, which means a quarrel.

The Irish name for the Milky Way is **Claí Mór na Réaltaí**, which translates literally as the big fence/ditch of stars. Another Irish name for the Milky Way is **Bealach na Bó Finne** (way of the fair cow). The constellation Orion is **An Saighduir Mór** (the big archer). The Irish for asteroid is the unlovely **astaróideach**, but **réalta mhongach** (long-haired star) is a word for comet.

When the stars go out, you might catch the dawning light: **fáinne an lae** (ring of the day).

In Irish, the gloaming, itself a lovely and underused word for the mixture of daylight and nightfall in the evening sky, is **amhdorchacht** (literally, uncooked darkness). **Tá an lá ag síneadh** means that it's getting dark later; literally, the day is stretching. This is, I understand, the origin of 'a grand stretch in the evening'. **Dearglach** refers to the beautiful red glow in the morning or evening skies.

Breacaimsir is a word for weather that is neither very good nor very bad. **Breac** means mixed or patchy and can refer to tartan patterns, as well as being the Irish word for trout. *Breacaimsir* is the best trout-fishing weather, I'm told! On a hotter day, you might see a **bruithleachán**; this means someone who sweats profusely. Speaking of sweat...

Allas is the Irish word for sweat.

Allas Muire (Mary's sweat) is St John's Wort.

Allas an Diabhail (devil's sweat) is a wee brat.

Fústar means fidget/fuss; this is the origin of foostering in English. One who foosters might be described as a **fústaire**. The Irish word for poltroon (itself a sadly neglected word) is **scraiste**. A wharf rat is **scraiste cé** – literally, quay poltroon.

Séanas means the gap between front teeth. **Ladhar**, on the other hand, means the gap between fingers or toes. An inability to grab things because your fingers are freezing is **sliopach**. This could affect your ability to play cards; the Irish for the ace of diamonds is **súil na muice**, which translates literally as the pig's eye. The Irish for the ace of hearts is **an banbh** (literally the piglet).

Binnghlórach is the Irish word for having a lovely voice, a word that could be used to describe someone from the beautiful county of Antrim. On a completely unrelated note, **áibhirseoireacht** means being thran ('thran' is an Antrim expression meaning to be wilfully disagreeable and uncooperative).

Aduantas doesn't have an equivalent word in English; it means the sensation of being in unfamiliar surroundings. This won't bother someone who's **guasach**, which means adventurous and danger-loving. Similarly, a person who is **so-ranna** would be able to overcome this feeling. **So-ranna** also doesn't have an exact match in English but is close to the French word **sortable**: the quality of a person who can be taken anywhere without fear of making a show of you. The opposite of **so-ranna** would be **do-ranna**: peevish, sour-minded or a bit socially awkward (and therefore likely to make a show of you).

Teach saolta means a respectable house. A **teach aolta** is a whitewashed house (which may or may not be respectable). The intriguing simile **chomh neamhnaofa le doras tigh ósta i nGaillimh** means 'as unholy as the door of a hostelry in Galway'.

There's no exact English word for **plámás** – it's often translated as to flatter, but also means just telling someone what they want to hear.

A speedbump is **uchtóg mhoillithe** (pausing or delaying bump). **Moilliu** can mean to dwell on a note in music. The Irish for baby shower is **cóisir réamhbhreithe**, which translates literally as pre-birth party.

The Irish word for trying to talk while bawling is **plobaireacht**. The opposite to this sad state of affairs would be giggling; **sciotar** is Irish for a giggle. Skimming stones across water is **sciotar uisce a dhéanamh**. Continuing with this watery theme, the verb **saibhseáil** means to dip something long into water to measure its depth; it may also mean to check or test something in general.

City dwellers aren't as connected with the animal world as they once were, so it's logical that numerous lost words refer to such connections. The verb **cleiteáil** means feather-plucking. It may also refer to a trouncing in a match, election, fight or debate (**fuair sé a chleiteáil**). **Lúrapóg lárapóg** is an onomatopoeic phrase representing the sound of a galloping horse, roughly equivalent to clip-clop in English. **Driuch** means a creepy feeling, like a rat has scurried over your grave.

More recognized as part of place names than a word in its own right, **ráth** means a ring fort, such as those once found in places such as Rathmines and Rathangan. However, it may also mean a shoal of fish (I love the idea of a shoal of fish being a fish fort). The phrase for forming a queue is **dul i scuaine**; **scuaine** can mean a hive or flock as well as a queue.

Ainle is a *recherché* word for a squirrel (used figuratively for a brat) and **áinle** means a swallow. Surely they're connected to **ainligh**, which means to hold steady against strong winds or currents. Speaking of weather, the Irish word for the sound of raindrops hitting the roof is **clagarnach**.

As well as meaning heavily pregnant, **leatromach** can mean unbalanced or lopsided. **Grá leatromach** means unrequited love. Sadly, these are sometimes connected.

Botún means a goose's stomach and may be a synecdoche for a plump gosling. However, it's usually used to refer to a cock-up. It may also refer to a farrier's knife, an unfledged bird or a mistake that cannot be undone. Speaking of mistakes that cannot be undone, the Irish word **cipín** may also refer to the instruments used when performing a castration (as well as its general meaning, a little stick)... and, possibly hinting at the final outcome of this procedure, the Irish word for a scrotum, **bosán**, may also mean a purse and a **striopadán** is a thing that hangs limp.

The handy word **asclán** means anything that might be carried under one arm (derived from **ascaill**, an armpit). Another term that doesn't have a direct match in English is **tónacán**, which means fidgeting in your seat (or sitting uneasily) – from **tóin**, meaning bottom.

Another of the numerous words for large-bottomed is **tiarpach**. It's derived from **tiarpa**, which can mean a heap or load... or an arse.

Blasachtach means to taste-test food. It may also mean to lick one's lips in anticipation. The Irish equivalent of a storm in a teacup is **cogadh na sifíní** (literally, war of the straws/stems). **Maológ** is the Irish word for the amount over the brim that a vessel (such as a sugar bowl) has been filled with.

Stráisiún doesn't have a direct equivalent in English; it means an unduly protracted visit. Someone who might engage in such a practice might be a **lorgánta** – a person fond of warming their shins (literally and/or figuratively).

A Fada Can Make All the Difference

Lagar	weakness, depression
Lágar	lager beer (one can lead to the other...)
Leacht	a grave mound
Léacht	a lecture
Leamh	impotent/sarcastic
Léamh	reading
Leann	ale or beer
Léann	learning
Camasach	having serpentine creeks
Cámasach	pretentious, quick to find fault in others
Oil	educate, train or reproach
Óil*	cheek
Airceach	voracious or needy
Aircéach	in geology, pertaining to rocks of the Archaeozoic portion of the Precambrian era
Romainis	Romani
Rómáinis	Romanian

* More commonly a grammatical form of *ól*, to drink.

The versatile word **síogaíocht** can mean fading away or gossip-mongering (**síog** is a streak, stripe or strikethrough). Speaking of stripes, the Irish for a zebra crossing is **trasrian síogach** – literally, a stripey crossing.

OUR WORDS II

The Great *Feamainn*:
Irish, Seaweed and the Deep

Ireland never had a myth of babies being delivered by
storks; the old story (in Kerry, anyway) was that they
were found in seaweed – this is discussed in the introduction to *Jimin Maire Thaidg*, when the protagonist wanders
the beach to see if he can find any himself. Beyond the
euphemisms parents use to describe reproduction to
children, seaweed had an important place in Irish life
for centuries. There's a poem by Aidan Matthews called
'The Death of Irish' that expresses the decline of *Gaeilge*
as the language's thirty-one words for seaweed whitening
on the shore. Neatly put. Like poetry, good manners and
romance, the Irish language has been declared dead or
dying for most of its existence. So it goes; we've all been
part of that conversation and so few of us have had our
minds changed. However, the existence of so many words
for seaweed – inevitably drawing comparisons to tales

of the Inuit and their languages"* words for snow – is an often-overlooked phenomenon.

Feamainn is the general term for seaweed and **glasarnacht** is a general term for water plants. **Turscar** is more specific; it means ugly, dead seaweed that the sea has abandoned on the shore. Cleverly, this is also the Irish word for spam email.

Anyone who has seen the film or the play *The Field* will remember how seaweed was used as fertilizer –'God made the world, but we made the field'.

* The original story about there being many Inuit words for snow didn't take account of the number of distinct Inuit languages and dialects. The thrust of the point – that circumstances influence vocabulary – still stands, though.

Spogán (or **slobán**) is a sort of seaweed that grows at the bottom of the ocean and is dredged up to be used to improve soil. **Racálach** is cast-up seaweed, the kind that might be collected by a **rácálaí**, a raker.

Stiallach is a word in Irish for tearing things into shreds or strips. It is also the descriptive name of a kind of seaweed used for making kelp and fertilizer. **Ceilp**, as its name suggests, is that variety that is called kelp in English. Similar to kelp is **coirleach** (**laminaria digitata**) and **copóg na gcloch** (stone's ear).

Cadamán and **barrchonlach** both refer particularly to the seaweed found on the upper part of the beach. On the other side of the shoreline would be **raibh**, floating seaweed. Not to be confused with **go raibh maith agat** (which means 'thank you').

Duileasc (also called **rapán**) is the variety of seaweed that's known as dulse in English. Another name for it is **creathnach**, which also means terrifying. **Lústrach** means withered seaweed, but can also mean obsequious. **Cáith-leach** is a kind of light seaweed, but can also mean phlegm.

Carraigín is, obviously, the variety known as carrageen moss in English. **Dúlamán** is the kind made popular in a song by Clannad; it may also mean a fool.

Féar gliomach translates literally as lobster grass, and describes long ribbons of seaweed. **Glasán** is sea lettuce (**Ulva lactuca** if you want to be all fancy about it). **Glasán** may also mean a finch or a bell. **Fuip**, as well as meaning a whip, is a tangled variety of seaweed. Adorably, **fuipín** is the word for a puffin chick. Speaking of puffins, **soipíneach** is the Irish word for nest but can also mean a heap of seaweed.

Leathach, which also means two-parted, is a kind of broad seaweed. Another helpfully descriptive name is **bhuilgéas**, which also means a blister. And don't forget about **casóg**, which also means jacket.

Scotach means tufted seaweed; a **bodóg** is a tuft of seaweed, but also can mean a heifer. While we're on a bovine theme, **bhó shleaidighe** (cows of sea lettuce) are edible seaweeds growing on rocks. The general term is **sleaidí** (*Monostroma grevillei*).

Rúscán is a strip of bark, or a vessel made of bark. It is also the name of a tough varietal of seaweed. **Múrach** can mean either brittle seaweed or fine clay. **Triopán** (or **torpán**) is a black edible seaweed.

Lóch is light seaweed, chaff, marshgrass or worthless stuff – not to be confused with **loch**, which means a lake. **Rualach** is the pretty variety of seaweed known as sea lace in English.

Sraoilleach is a form of the word **sraoill** which means to flog, scourge, tear or flagellate; a **duine sraoilleach** would be an utterly bedraggled person. As you can probably work out, seaweed described as **scraoilleach** is a scrappy, raggy growth with the appearance of beggar's rags.

Every Irish child looks forward to **milseán** – the Irish word for sweets. They may not be quite so effusive about **milseán mara**, the kind of maritime fauna that the experts refer to as **saccharina lattisima**. The genus known as *Porphyra purpurea* in Latin is simply called **sleabhach** in Irish, which means droopy or limp.

With such a plethora of words for seaweed, you won't be surprised to hear that there are some colourful expressions for aquatic life too. Here's a sample:

Smugairle* róin	jellyfish	literally, seal snot†
Mathair súigh	squid	suck-mother
Cíoch charraige	sea anemone	rock boob
Crosán	starfish	jester or mimic
Hata an tsagairt	sea anemone	priest's hat

---

* *Smugairle* can mean spit or snot. A *smugarlach* is a person whose nose is always running.

•

† The Icelandic word for jellyfish is *marglytta*, literally translating as sea glitter. The Portuguese is *aqua viva*, living water.

Cac ar leicín	sea anemone	shite on a little flat stone
Gráinneog thrá	sea urchin	beach hedgehog
Carbhán carraige	sea urchin	rock caravan

If you think those names are ridiculous, imagine what a fisherman in Galway one hundred years ago would've thought of the word anemone.

A Fada Can Make All the Difference

Tonóg	a duck
Tónóg	a small bottom
Sian	whine or squeal
Sián	fairy mound
Peileacán	a pelican
Péileacán*	butterfly (more usually féileacán)
Goraí	a goal
Góraí	a hatching hen (or a similarly impatient person)
Cátúil	esteemed, honoured
Catúil	feline
Béar	a bear
Beár	a bar

* This can also refer to the intangible quality that is removed from someone when they're beaten in a fight or argument – *bhí said ag brú na péileacáin as a chéile* means 'they were beating the shite out of each other'.

Glam	**a bark or howl**
Glám	grab or clutch
Séad	**a way, course or path ... or treasured object**
Sead	a nest ... or, as a verb, to squirt/ejaculate
Con	**hound (variation of cú)**
Cón	cone
Braiteach	**perceptive or alert**
Bráiteach	shoaling ground
Feimineach	**feminist**
Feimíneach	tail-chewing animal
Máige	**paw (genitive of mág)**
Maige	tilted or cocked (gen. of maig)
Fair	**(to keep) watch**
Fáir	a hen's nest ... or sunrise
Readán	**pipe or reed**
Réadán	woodworm

PEOPLE AND OTHER ANIMALS

An **athchainteach** person is cheeky and has tales to tell... as opposed to someone **eireaballach**, who has a tail and may not be cheeky at all.

The Irish word for wild, **fiata**, also means shy. This is one of my favourite double meanings in Irish; it's touchingly respectful of the creatures we share the planet with. Similarly, the Irish for wolf is **mac tíre**, which translates literally as son of the country, showing an acceptance of the place wolves have in the wild. On the other hand, a **meiltire** is someone who can't or won't shut up. It's easy to remember because they give you a brain melter (*meiltire*) of a headache.

See if you can spot a trend in this list:

Madra uisce	otter	water dog
Madra crainn	squirrel	tree dog
Madra allta	wolf	wild dog

Madra rua	fox	red dog
Madraí bána	bee larvae	white dogs
Madra mara	seal	sea dog
Madra taoide	strong tide	tide dog

No prizes there; these are some hilariously literal animal names that seem almost infantile when set next to each other, and an uninformed browser might draw conclusions about the merit of the entire language based on the lack of flair shown here. However, all these creatures have multiple names in the Irish language, ranging from the poetic to the sublime.

As well as beautiful names for animals, Irish also holds some dazzlingly precise names for people along the lines of **meiltire**... and then there are the overlaps between the two.

A **gastóg** is a smart, quick rejoinder or riposte. It can also mean a woman or girl with a talent for serving out such remarks.

The versatile word **dradaire** can mean a person with big teeth, a flirt, a chatterbox, a wimp or a smart alec... or a combination of these.

The Irish for starling is **druid**. The Irish for druid is **draoi**.

The Irish word **dúchan** means sadness or darkening – not to be confused with **dúchas**, which means heritage, hereditary right or instinct. A **madra dúchais** is a mad dog, one who has gone native (and possibly sad or dark).

The Irish for a boar is **torc**. The name of the Turk's Head on Parliament Street refers to a boar's head, not that of a citizen of Turkey. The Irish for a gerbil is **seirbil**, not to be confused with **Seirbis**, which means Serbian.

Interest on a loan is **gaimbín**; this is the origin of 'gombeen man', an unscrupulous moneylender. One of the Irish names for a raven, **fiach**, also means debt or a tooth. Another Irish name for a raven is **Dónall dubh** – literally black Daniel. A hairy caterpillar can be called **Dónall an chlúimh** (downy Daniel).

Gardaí	police
Gadaí	thief

Earc means a lizard and is not to be confused with **earcach**, which means a new (similarly green) recruit.

One of the Irish words for a giggler is **scigire**... not to be confused with **cigire**, meaning inspector. They don't giggle. **Fáilteoir** means receptionist – not to be confused with **áilteoir**, a practical joker (who may or may not also be a receptionist).

The versatile word **cleasaí** may mean an acrobat, an adventurer, an engineer, an intriguer, a leg-puller, a mountebank, a rogue, a schemer or a playful person or animal. Another word for mountebank is **gleacaí**, which can mean a wrestler, a gymnast, a trickster or a faker.

The Irish for sculptor is **dealbhóir**. **Dealbh** is a sculpture but can also mean bleak, destitute or empty.

The Irish for a knight is **ridire**. This also covers the title of a knighthood; for example, **An Ridire Bob Geldof** is Sir Bob Geldof. The Irish for Sir Mix-A-Lot would be **An Ridire Suaith-Go-Leor**.

The Irish for a turf cutter is **móinbhainteoir** – **bainteoir** means a reaper or digger, not to be confused with banter (**mionmhagadh**, tiny mockery).

The Irish for a libertarian is **liobraíoch**... not to be confused with **liobarnach**, which means hanging loose.

One of the Irish words for a tapeworm is **cailleach ghoile**, which translates bluntly as stomach nun. **Cailleach** can also mean a stump, a bundle, a nun, a precocious girl, a witch or a withered thing. Tapeworms are notoriously gluttonous; the word **airceach** can mean voracious or needy. This may or may not be connected to **arcán**, meaning piglet. Too old to be a piglet, too young to be a pig? It's called a **céis** in Irish. (**Céis** also means a small harp* and **céisliní** are tonsils.) **Mo céis breágh muice** is an old term of endearment from Dinneen's Dictionary which means my beautiful young pig. And a **mucachán** is a human being with characteristics more typically associated with a pig.

* The harp is an enduring symbol of Ireland; by way of coincidence, an old name for Ireland is *Muc-Inis*, pig island.

Contrary to the American phrase 'happy as a clam', the Irish word for a clam, **breallach**, can also mean unhappy, hapless, foolish or clumsy. However, as the full expression is 'happy as a clam at low tide' and actually refers to temporary, doomed, simple contentment, it all starts to make more sense. *Breallach* may also be used as an adjective to describe someone or something with clamlike lips.

The Irish for girth is **giorta**, not to be confused with **gorta**, which means hunger – be especially careful not to mix up **an Gorta Mór** (the Famine) with **an giorta mór** ('the big girth'). Soup is **anraith** – not to be confused with **anlaith**, which means tyrant. Soup, of course, has a particular significance in Irish memory, as certain people 'took soup' during the Famine. Taking soup meant not starving, but this came at the cost of accepting Protestant charity; the implication was that the price of soup was converting or abandoning Irish (people who use the English spelling of their name or drop the O in their surname are sometimes referred to as having taken soup). It is unclear from historical evidence if such demands were made on soup-takers and there is a widespread theory that this is a myth dating from the early days of the Free State; the first mention of soupers (**lucht anraithe**) in an Irish dictionary is in the 1926 edition of Dinneen.

One of the words for low-fat is **éadrom**; an **éadroman** is a balloon, air-filled vessel or a person who's a bit of a flake. Another word for low-fat is **beagmhéathrais** (literally, small of fat). Not to be confused with **beagmhaitheas**, uselessness. **Carán** is an Irish word for darling, not to be confused with **carrán**, which means the layer of thick scum on top of buttermilk. Although **im** means butter and **eagla** means fear, **imeagla** does not mean fear of butter. It means utter dread. Chewing gum is **salaid**, not to be confused with **sailéad**, which means salad. Careful what you order... Likewise, a child's potty is **áraisín**, not to be confused with a raisin.

A surname in Irish beginning with *Ní* indicates that the bearer is an *iníon*, a daughter of the family – as opposed to Ó (son of) or *Uí* (wife of).

The Irish for daughter is **iníon*** – not to be confused with onion, a vegetable worn in France but eaten elsewhere.

An Úcráin, meaning Ukraine, is not to be confused with **cráin**, which means a female pig. The Irish for queen bee is **cráinbheach**, which translates literally as sow bee. Not quite as fabulous. While the Irish term may superficially seem less respectful than the English one, it should be mentioned that bees had a significant place in pre-Norman Ireland, when they were regarded as mysterious, wise and symbolic of the natural world's inherent orderliness and willingness to punish anyone who disrupts it. This is illustrated by the *seanfhocal trí ní is deacair a thuiscint: intleacht na mban, obair na mbeach, teacht agus imeacht na taoide*, which means 'the three things hardest to understand: the minds of women, the work of bees and the comings and goings of the tide'. The importance of bees led to some highly-specific bee-related words: **beachaire** can mean beehive or a beekeeper, a swarm of bees (secured to the hive) is a **slaod** (which can also mean heavy layers) or **saithe**, a second swarm of bees is known as **mac-shaithe** and a swarm of bees that is additional to the hive's secured swarm is a **smearaighe**.

Seilmideáil means dawdling, going at a snail's pace (from **seilide**, a snail).

Stadhan doesn't have an exact match in English; it means a flock of birds gathered above a shoal of fish. The adjective **faoileánach** describes a place with an abundance of seagulls. The Irish for seagull is **faoileán**, which is often translated literally as wolf bird. If someone has seagull-esque grace, you could describe them as **faoileanda**. As for less objectionable birds, **lasair choille** (flame of the wood/ forest) is one of the more dramatic names for a goldfinch – not to be confused with **lasairéan**, which means flamingo (literally, flame bird).* A sparrow is **gealbhan** (bright

* I always remember this one because my daughter's name is Lasairíona.

white). Birds are beloved for their music; the Irish for jazz is **snag-cheol** and a woodpecker is **snag darach**.

Ulchabhán, owl, translates literally as white beard. Another expression for owl is **scréachóg reilige**, which translates as shrill graveyard bird. **Ceann cait** (literally cat head) is the Irish for a certain kind of owl, one whose head looks a little bit like a cat's.

It's tempting to think that there's a link between the Russian for puppy (**schenok**) and the Irish for fox (**sionnach**), but I think it just might be one of life's wonderful coincidences – like the Vietnamese for beef, *bo*, being almost identical to the Irish for a cow.

A **fáinneoir** is someone who rings animals. That is to say, someone who puts rings on their noses. It does not (necessarily) mean someone who rings animals up on the phone. A **cinnire** (a word some of you will remember from the Gaeltacht) is someone who leads an animal by the head.

Colann	A one-year-old heifer
Ceartaos	A two-year-old heifer
Samhaisc	A three-to-four-year-old heifer

The Irish for a dragonfly is **snáthaid mhór**, which translates literally as big needle. The name for a cranefly is even better: **snáthaid an diabhail** (devil's needle). The Irish word for a pug is **smutmhadra**.

The word **eas** can mean a waterfall or a stoat. **Torann easa** means the roar of a waterfall (or possibly the roar of a stoat, I suppose) . . .*

The Irish word for a mole (on the skin, not *The Wind in the Willows* kind) is **ball dobhráin**, which translates literally as an otter spot. An otter is **dobharchú**, which translates literally as water hound or flood hound. This could be confused with the word for hippopotamus, **dobhareach** – literally, a flood-horse. An evil-doing hippo would be **dobhareach dobheartach**.

A **sramachán** is a bleary-eyed person, not to be confused with a **sramaide**, which means a slimy, sneaky person or animal.

Éan péan is the old Irish nickname for a magpie. **Éan** means bird; **péan** doesn't mean anything, but rhymes. Bird pird? A **mearaitheoir** is someone who infuriates you with distractions and interruptions.

The Irish for polar bear is **béar bán**, which translates literally as white bear.

* In the interest of accuracy, I should point out that *eas* (waterfall) is masculine and *eas* (stoat) is feminine; they're not the same word.

The Irish word **eallach**, meaning goods or cattle, is not to be confused with the adjective **ealach** (frequented or enjoyed by swans). **Spréidh/Spré** can mean cattle, fortune or dowry.

The Irish word **gíománach** means a henchman, coachman or surly churl – not to be confused with **gormánach**, an adolescent seal that has shed its cute, white baby-fur … and is no longer quite so adorable.

Rón	a seal (can also mean horsehair)
Rón mór	a sea lion (literally a big seal)
Rónadóir	one who makes and sells fur products

Rónadóir may also mean a feather merchant – as opposed to a **clúmhadóir**, who is merely a feather dealer.

The Irish word **searc** means love – not to be confused with shark, a misunderstood fish. A blue shark is **craosaire gorm**, which translates literally as blue glutton. Sharks, like bats, get a bad rap in films. The simile **chomh sámh le liamhán gréine** means 'as chilled out as a basking shark'.

One of the Irish names for a lobster is **gliomach Spáinneach**, which literally translates as Spanish lobster. A porpoise is **muc mhara** – literally, a sea pig. A **líbíneach** is someone or something that is dripping wet. A **ribe róibéis** is a shrimp… not to be confused with **ribe caithre**, a pubic hair.

A cloud is **scamall** – not to be confused with **camall**, which means a camel.

Here are some words to describe certain categories of people, who may or may not be as civilized as the animals we have considered so far in this chapter.

A **lámhacánaí** is someone (usually a baby, but sometimes a wacky adult or a thief) who moves around on their hands and knees.

A **falcaire** is a potato that's hollow in the middle. It can also mean a deceitful person. A **sliomach** is a bad potato, one that cannot be eaten for one reason or another. It can also mean a useless person.

The word **slámálaí** can mean a plucker, an untidy worker or a wasteful person prone to impecuniousness. Everybody knows one. A **smearachálaí** (a greaser or smearer) is someone who does messy work.

The word **cnagadán** means a tough little man – this comes from **cnag**, a knock, blow, strike or cracking sound.

The Irish for a curly-haired person is **catachán**.

Angarais means a clumsy, awkward, out-of-shape animal or person.

A **stríocálaí** is someone who makes a valiant effort in spite of a lack of skill.

CUIMILT FAOI DHEIS

Irish Today

The first holiday Erin and I took together was to Venice. It's a magical city, and you don't need to be an art nerd like I am to fall in love with it. One of the especially enchanting things about it is the way, like Bruges or Pompeii, it has been preserved as it was at a moment in time. For Venice, it was the moment when it was the trade gateway between Europe and the Near East, a point of cultural contact that led to the invention of banking, establishing the secular patronage of art that kick-started the Renaissance. However, if you think about that for long enough, you realize that this moment in time was actually when it stopped changing and was no longer the commercial hub where new ideas were born.

The Italian government spends a lot of money preserving Venice, which also means that certain modern municipal comforts have to be relinquished. Outside the old town, there's a swathe of urban sprawl where normal business happens. Almost as a counterbalance to the endeavours to preserve old Venice, it seems that anything goes in this grim hinterland, which only exists to give breathing room to the city that must not change.

What is it like to live in an antique?

Sometimes I think that the Irish language is a little bit like Venice; it's beautiful, it's ours, and destroying it to make room for something bland that you could get anywhere else in the world just doesn't make sense. People who come here from faraway have expectations about it. But people need to live and work. Can canals made for gondolas handle motorboats? Where do you put the electricity and broadband cables? If nothing new is built, where do the new people live?

Venice, Bruges and Pompeii all had their brakes pulled sharply (like the Irish language), but other cities – Paris, Barcelona, Istanbul – have found ways to streamline change and modernity around the treasures of the past. What's their secret – other than being wealthy?

Among the rules that the *Oxford English Dictionary* has governing the inclusion of new words is a stipulation that the new word must be in common use for five years. The implication of this is, of course, that the dictionary is not an accurate reflection of words in common use. The guardians of the lexicon are fearful that dreck such as *selfie, cowabunga* and *nimby* might darken the august pages that contain proper words like *aginbite, bailiwick* and *valetudinarian* unless a triage or quarantine is in place. Proper, respectable people like proper, respectable words for their proper, respectable language, words that are relevant to them.

The thing is that new words and innovation in language tend to come from groups of people who (to significantly varying degrees) don't fit into this relevance – teenage girls, gay people, minorities, the poor, foreigners, 'the regions', young – people who are, by implication, not proper. For an unhappy chunk of history, Irish people were such a group in America and the United Kingdom. It's a source of sly pride here that our outsider status gave us a unique perspective which, combined with an irreverent and detached attitude to the English language, created some of the greatest literature the planet has ever been blessed with. So why is it so hard to accept that disruptive creativity in Irish? For some people, Irish is a ceremonial language to be kept behind a velvet rope and admired, with alarm bells to ring if anyone attempts to change (or even touch) it.

Consider this – the Irish word **meabhlach** means attractive, colourable or seductive. The dictionary advises us that this may also mean shameful or disgraceful – who thinks like that anymore?

Despite being perceived as a pillar of Official Ireland, *Gaeilge* has become a big part of counterculture here; in an era of political and social consensus, the Irish-language media outlets have promoted different voices and perspectives. Irish-language writing escaped the puritanical excesses of the censors in the middle of the twentieth century; in some instances (like Merriman's *The Midnight Court**) the English translation was banned but the Irish version was available.

In this chapter I will share with you some words which give a flavour

* Brian Merriman (1747–1805) is famous for a single work, *Cúirt an Mheán Oíche* (The Midnight Court), an extended verse in which a narrator is presented with the machinations of a supernatural courtroom where opinions are offered on infidelity, divorce and the ethics surrounding young priests being able to marry.

of the Irish enjoyed in the first quarter of the twenty-first century.

Sometimes people suggest neologisms to me. One of the better ones I've heard is **focras** for 'hangry', based on the following logic: (hungry and angry) = **focras** (**fearg** and **ocras**). **Ubhmeathán** was suggested to me as a timely Irish word for a Twitter troll – it translates literally as egg coward. (The Irish for egg is **ubh** and **meathán** is one of a number of words for coward, and can also mean a sapling or a young fragile plant, one that appears spineless). **Slogfhéachaint** (literally, swallow watching) was suggested as an Irish translation for binge watching. **Boscailt** was offered too as a translation of the word phrase 'wide-on'. Lovely! *

Earworm (itself a recent borrowing from German) was translated on TG4† as **éistphéist** (**éist**, listen; **péist**, worm or pest), which is so clever and rhyming that it would easily make you believe that the German and English words must have come later.‡

Although the Irish for lunch is **lón**, somebody decided that brunch should be translated as **bróinse**. If the English form had been followed faithfully, the **br-** in **bricfeásta** and the **-ón** in **lón** would leave us with **brón**, which means sadness. If we're going to be having a glass of prosecco with our rashers and sausages and huevos rancheros, we shouldn't be sad.

* A *neamhfhobhrísteoir* is someone who declines (or omits) to wear underpants – another wonderful suggestion I received since setting up @theirishfor. How did we ever speak to each other without it?

† Specifically, this translation was used in the dubbed version of *Spongebob Squarepants*.

‡ Continuing the Spongebob theme, the Irish for jester or mimic, *crosán*, also means starfish.

Speaking of brunch, global hipster trends have not passed Ireland by, especially in Galway city, the Liberties (and the greater Dublin 8 area) and Stoneybatter. A defining characteristic of this movement (as described in *Stuff White People Like*) is an enthusiasm for authenticity, as well as a dollop of middle-class guilt. In this sense, urban **gaeilgeoirs** have been hipsters for years.

But what do we call hipsters in Irish? **Gaige na maige** (literally, a swaggering fop or tilted dandy) has the advantage of already being on record – it's listed in Dinneen's dictionary, so why make a new word when an old one will do? Other pre-existing candidate words include **beadaí** (more precisely meaning foodie rather than a general hipster, even though there's an overlap), **éigsín** (a student of poetry, but also a bad poet, a superficial scholar or an annoying self-described creative type) and, of course, **lucht cathrach** – city people.

Féasóg	beard§
Rothar stadghléasra	fixed gear bike (or possibly **ficsí**)
Feoilséantóir	vegetarian (this translates literally as meat denier)

§ No, this doesn't mean young face – *féas* means coarse hair. Another word for a beard is *ulcha*; an *ulchabhán*, literally a white beard, is one of the Irish words for an owl. *Amhulchach* means beardless (or owl-less, probably).

Tatú tattoo

Siopa ceirníní record store

The Irish word **gotha** means a pose or affectation; it doesn't necessarily or exclusively refer to goths. Oh, and notions – especially notions above one's station – would be **fuadar ard**. (**Leath-thuairim** means notion in its 'vague idea' sense as opposed to its 'it's far from feng shui ye were raised' sense.)

The Irish for a gymnasium is **áras gleacaíocht**a. Interestingly, a gallows is **garma gleacaíochta**. I look forward to them both about as much. **Bogshodar**, to jog, translates literally as soft trot, invoking memories of the charming expression 'bogtrotter'.

The Irish word for a bra, **cíochbheart**, translates literally as breast garment. The Irish for underpants is **fobríste**, not to be confused with **dobhriste**, which means sacred. A manicure is **lámh-mhaisiú**, which translates as hand decoration. A loofah is **lúfach**, not to be confused with **líofa**, which can mean fluent or sharpened.

The Irish for a hairdresser is **gruagaire** – not to be confused with **guagaire**, an odd and unpredictable soul. Confusingly, the Irish word **bob** can mean a long fringe (or bangs, as they say in the States).

The Irish for the creaking of shoes is **díoscadh bróg** – not to be confused, I'm afraid, with disco shoes.

A cocktail is **manglam** – this may also mean a hodgepodge, a heterogeneous mixture or a sleazy person. A cosmopolitan is **iltíreach**, which translates literally as of many lands. Nowadays we only think of the cosmopolitan as the cocktail, but the original meaning was a Communist – especially a Trotskyite intent on spreading the Revolution abroad. The naming of the cocktail was a cheeky reference to its red colour and (Russian) vodka content. The fact that the USSR called their astronauts cosmonauts complemented this. This evolution of a word – where a secondary meaning takes precedence over a primary one that gradually falls out of use – has implications for translation if the two languages in question are moving in different directions.

Sometimes people take time out of their day to poke fun at Irish, and this inevitably leads to them identifying inelegant word borrowings from English, especially ones which refer to some recent invention or concept. **Léasar** is the Irish word for laser, and it's an instructive example of how not to do loanwords.

In English, laser is an acronym for Light Amplification by Stimulated Emission of Radiation. I'd take the view that you either translate the sentence and make a new acronym (SASAR, possibly), lift the English spelling as it is, or come up with a new word entirely that conveys the meaning consistently with the flow of Irish. Forcing the English word to dress up as an Irish one without regard for meaning seems to be the least wonderful option. Also, the Irish for a flame is **lasair**. A missed opportunity.

On the other hand, **turscar** is the Irish word for email spam, and rocks in all the ways **léasar** cannot. Instead of just saying **spám** or something, they found an old term for disgusting, dead seaweed that had been cast upon the shore by an uncaring sea and used it as the Irish word for unwelcome emails. With language, meaning can lead the way and there's no need for a new word when there's a perfectly good one in the toolkit.

In 2003, Donald Rumsfeld hubristically referred to the invasion of Iraq as a 'cakewalk', meaning that it'd be easy-peasy. Linguists duly decided to focus on his choice of words (rather than his views on the wisdom of starting a war) and pointed out that cakewalk could be viewed as offensive – it was a dance in the American South in the eighteenth century, which was an imitation by white slave-owners of a dance they observed slaves performing. What's especially interesting about this is that the dance performed by the slaves (the pre-cakewalk) was itself a mocking imitation of the overly courtly dances they had witnessed their masters enjoying.

Like two tilted mirrors reflecting each other, cultures in proximity exchange moves, ideas and words back and forth, and there are many cakewalks in the dictionary, like eejit, **slíbhín** or smithereens.

A dictionary is, like a newspaper or the *Guinness Book of Records*, a snapshot of a moment in time. Words are like passengers on a bus (one of those European buses that can stretch in the middle during busy periods) where passengers are getting on and off all the time, and a dictionary just captures a snapshot. This is especially true in lesser-used languages like Irish, where new editions of the official dictionary are published occasionally rather than every single year; the 1977 Ó Dónaill *Foclóir*, for example, doesn't include the modern use of *craic* as meaning highly informal fun or merriment. It does, however, suggest that craic can mean conversation or chat, as well as being an adjective to describe a crazy person; by the '90s, these meanings had merged. Given the popularity of crack cocaine in larger

American cities at the time, this loanword caused less confusion in writing when the Irish spelling was used.

New words are suspicious creatures – we're not always sure where they have come from or what they want. You simply don't know where they've been.

 Cool Story, Bro

Is the 'official' suspicion towards new words reasonable? One complaint is that these new words are volatile things. Consider, for example, the word bro. It is, plainly, an abbreviation of brother. Many people have brothers, myself included. However, in this particular context it owes much to the African-American dialects – its use in religious congregations as a term of kinship and solidarity and how this trickled down into soul music and beyond. Brother was never used in Ireland in this way. The popularity of the shortened version slid into mainstream English on foot of its use in hip-hop in the '80s. Its appropriation by white teenagers (who grew up to be white adults) contributed to its tilting away from this meaning. While words like dude evolved to become less gender specific, the emphasis of bro moved from black male camaraderie to male camaraderie. So much so, in fact, that now bro is synonymous with white middle-class chauvinists rather than southern Baptists or soul musicians. So it goes – another cakewalk.

Think about all the layers of meaning in a word like bro for a moment, and how those alternate meanings at different times inform each other. Now imagine translating it.

Sticking with the same example, the Irish word for brother is **dearthái r.** So, what should the Irish for bro be? This raises all sorts of practical questions.

Firstly, is the word required in the language at all? This is a popular question with the 'why is this news' brigade. Even so, this can be a valid point; one language shouldn't dictate the content of another. Secondly, does a word with an equivalent meaning already exist in Irish? If this is the case, then everybody wins. **Seomra** means room and **bainne** means milk and nobody need be confused. With new words, it's rarely that simple.

We then have the following options:

1. *Take it in, as is* (bro). Given that this word's use in Hiberno-English contains an intentional nod to its American origins, it's not outrageous to do the same in Irish. This would be consistent with the way verboten and ennui are used in English; it is understood that forbidden and boredom are already in the vocabulary but the associations carried by the German and French forms flavour the meaning. This is the 'well-done steak' option – frowned upon by the connoisseur, but popular with punters.

2. *Take it in, but adjust the spelling to match the norms of Irish* (**bró**). This reasonable compromise provokes groans from both laymen and experts (it's the 'medium steak' option), but it's the normal practice in other European languages.

3. *Look at the components of the word and translate them* (abbreviate **deartháir** to **der**, maybe?) This is the medium-rare option, and gives the option of an authentic-sounding word that keeps *Gaeilge*'s dignity intact by not sounding too English. Consider if the Irish word for a dentist, **fiaclóir**,

(which finds matching Irish elements to *dent-* [tooth] and *-ist* [practitioner]) was **deántiast** or something like that and you'll see why. Similarly, as **lag** means weakness and the letter **J** is frowned upon, jetlag is translated as **tuirse aerthurais**, which translates literally as air-trip fatigue – forcing the term into Irish spelling norms just wouldn't work here. Like a medium-rare steak, it can be ruined in a split second.

Cnó cócó, the Irish for coconut, takes a little from option two and a little from option three.

4. *Don't take it in, but find the closest existing word with the same meaning* (a **mhac** is an informal way of addressing a male peer or lackey equivalent to bro). This is the steak tartare – it hasn't gone near the translator's frying pan, but it has been carefully sliced. It only works with the best quality meat, and even then, you wouldn't want to eat steak tartare every day.

5. *Consider the history and intended meaning of the word.* The rare steak option (perfectly seared on the outside and beautifully pink on the inside) is possible in translation with an intimate and creative knowledge of both languages. For example, **seomra** means a room (such as a bedroom) but does not share room's other meaning (the abstract concept of available space). *Seomra* comes from *chambre* in French, which also means room but entered English as chamber. Some of chamber's English meanings are covered by *seomra* (burial chamber – *seomra*

adhlachtha) but some aren't (gun chamber – **cuasán**). In this light, could the myriad meanings of bro be better served by separate words?

Examples of this include the wonderfully alliterative translation of agony aunt, **colúnaí crá croí**, which translates literally as heartache columnist, but keeps the alliteration of the original English term. Flashmob is **tobshlua** (literally, quick crowd) and cheerleader is **gárthóir molta** (literally, praise screamer). Finally, a high five is **bosa in airde** (palms high).

To understand the etymological journey that a word took to reach its English shape, and to recreate it, is like linguistic ballet and, like ballet, can baffle many. But if a rhyme or a double meaning can be replicated in translation, or if a droll aside can be inferred, or if the new term is just beautifully put, then something wonderful has happened.

People like new stuff, and new things need names. Sometimes the new thing is from another country and already has a name. If this is the case, then we have one less job to do. This is especially the case with food, where English speakers will consume sushi, sashimi, fajitas, cappuccinos and falafels without thinking to concoct authentically Anglophone new names for them. Then again, English isn't fighting for its existence in the same way.

Generally speaking, every new word arrives in Irish from another language, and that language is generally English. We're not threatened by Japanese or Spanish, so there's less of a panic to translate these loanwords (options one or two generally apply). However, English loanwords in Irish are perceived to stand in mockery of the Republic's 'noble objective', and must be kicked into shape.

Not all English comes from England, but it's all 'English' when it comes near the **teanga** – even if it's coming from Ireland's thirty-third county, New South Wales. One of the more pleasant impacts of Hiberno-Australian relations in the past decade has been the introduction of the flat white to Ireland. But how should this be translated into Irish?

First of all, a literal translator has to deal with the fact that flat white has two adjectives in search of a noun. A flat white what? Can grammatically correct Irish be salvaged from a grammatically incorrect English phrase? Secondly, what exactly is meant by flat? I put this to the floor on Twitter with a few suggestions:

Bán mín	a literal translation
Cothrom bán	a different literal translation
Cothromín	little flat
Báinín	little white
Caife Astráileach	a nod to the flat white's origins
Caife nóisín	'notiony' coffee

The first two literal terms have their advantages, although **Bán mín** is a bit more elegant – it matches the syllable count of the original English term. My impression is that a tourist in the Gaeltacht would recognize **Caife Astráileach** as being a flat white before the others. **Nóisín** isn't good Irish; it's a retrofitting of notions that's been specifically designed to rhyme with Róisín to tease girls with that name. However, this is exactly the kind of knowing, self-deprecating wordplay that coffee-slurping urbanites enjoy. However, my favourite is **báinín** – it accurately describes the product (a small coffee with milk), but even more impressively, it nods to an existing coffee-naming tradition. Just as cappuccinos were named in reference to the robes of cappucin monks, a *báinín* is a traditional woollen waistcoat in the West of Ireland.

Báinín won (insofar as Twitter polls have any bearing) but I'd be interested to see what *Conradh na Gaeilge**** think.

Closer to home, takeaways across Ireland were caught up with a new craze sweeping Ireland – the spice bag. Dublin's answer to the deep-fried Mars bar, the spicebag was a combination of chips, chicken strips, sliced peppers and curry sauce that proved to be greater than the sum of its parts. As it was born of this land, I felt that it required a name in Irish and offered some suggestions to the voting public on Twitter. As with flat white, a literal translation was problematic. After all, it is not a bag of spices and the bag itself is not spiced; a small amount of interpretation was required.

* *Conradh na Gaeilge* is the organization dedicated to promoting the Irish language and defending the rights of Irish speakers and Gaeltacht communities.

Mála spíosraí   the 'medium-rare' choice (following the existing form for spice box).

Spaighaisbag   the 'medium' option (following the sound).

Mangán blasta   this 'rare' suggestion anticipates concerns with the word spice and uses

blasta – tasty – instead. **Mangán** is also a less primary-school word for bag than **mála**.

Bia Átha Cliath a punning nod to the spice bag's origins, this means Dublin food.

Mála spíosraí turned out to be the term that people were most comfortable with.

⌗ Brexit – A Short History of a New Word ⌗

In 2016, voters in England and Wales decided to leave the European Union, and their majority was big enough to cancel out the fact that most voters in Northern Ireland, Scotland and London wanted to stay. This is ironic because the word Brexit itself, a portmanteau of Britain and exit,* ignores the fact that it was the United Kingdom (the political entity) leaving rather than Britain (an island that doesn't include Northern Ireland, which would be obliged to leave). Either way, the word caught on. But what would it be called in Irish?

This presented an immediate practical challenge to Irish speakers, particularly those working in Irish-language journalism: what do we call this thing? **Nuacht** on RTÉ went with **Breatimeacht**, which follows the Brexit portmanteau exactly; **Breatain** and **imeacht**. However, some speakers, concluding that the driving force for Brexit was English nationalism, suggested that **Sasanamach** (or **Sasamach**) might be more appropriate: **Sasanach** (English) and **amach** (out).

* The word Brexit followed the stylings of the incumbent term Grexit that referred to the possible ejection of Greece from the EU.

My suggestion – **Slán Bán Breathnach** (a pun on the name of the legendary broadcaster* and the words for Wales† and goodbye) – sadly never caught on.

Speaking of Brexit... the Irish for English is *Sasanach* but the Irish for the English language is **Béarla**. However, before *béarla* meant English it referred to speech (**béal** and **radh**) – especially highfalutin' talk. **Béarla na bhfileadh** refers to an artificial jargon once used by poets, and **Béarla féine** (the Speech of the Freemen) was an ancient legal language. Some who wish to maintain the distinction refer to the English language pointedly as **Sacs-Bhéarla** (English-English).

These discrete words for English and the English language in Irish hint at the scope of Englishness as a presence in Irish. The success of the project to anglicize Ireland seems like a *fait accompli* now, but was only achieved through years of persistence and one botched effort after

---

* Seán 'Bán' Breathnach is a legendary Irish-language broadcaster, best known for *Scaoil Amach An Bobailín*, a very respectable magazine show on RTÉ. Its name is an Irish phrase that means to cut loose and have fun (literally, release the tassel). However, this is also taken to mean 'peel back the foreskin and unleash the glans', explaining why a *Scaoil Amach An Bobailín* banner was confiscated from supporters at Croke Park in the '80s by a Garda who thought it was obscene.

† Wales is *An Bhreatain Bheag*; Great Britain is *An Bhreatain Mhór*. *Breatnach* means Welsh, or a Welsh person.

another; arguably it only succeeded because of the tragic accident of the Famine. It's as if someone spent years trying to cut a tree down and one day woke up to find it had been struck by a bolt of lightning. Sometimes I wonder if the people who give out about the state's expenditure on Irish-language projects ever wonder about the waste and cost involved in putting Irish on the back foot in the first place. I suspect that they rarely think about it at all.

Inevitably some transference occurred during this time. The Irish word for the particles projected by a smith's hammer is **smidiríní**, which entered English as smithereens. As the Irish for smith is **gabha**, smithereen is a rare word form which moved from English (smith) to Irish (**smidir** and diminutive suffix -**ín**) and then back to English again (smithereen).

While Irish readily accommodated English words, English (as it was spoken in Ireland and Anglophone countries with Irish communities) was also picking up words from Irish. The English word galore comes from **go leor**, meaning plenty (or enough). I'm told that smashing entered English from **is maith sin** (that's good) courtesy of Irish builders in England, and that 'so long' is derived from **slán**, goodbye. However, this opens up a can of worms...

There's Always One...

Believe it or not, people can predict the future. Not all the time and not often with the precision that would make it profitable, but I often think that the force that makes the world rotate is the collective daily sigh of 'I told you so'. I can predict the future within certain circumstances, none of which generate income or joy. Specifically, I know that if I state that if a word in English owes its origin to an Irish form, I will shortly be advised that I am wrong and that I am citing a disreputable, discredited source. My computer screen often steams up from the seething rage at the other end of the Internet.

Some years ago, a writer by the name of Daniel Cassidy gave the world a book called *How the Irish Invented Slang*, in which he put forth the theory that the Irish language had trickled through spoken English in the United States (plausibly enough) but that this influence had been intentionally erased by linguists with an anti-Irish agenda. He suggests that words like dig (in the context of 'can you dig it?') and jazz have their origins in Irish.

In addition to stating that words like jazz and dude came from Irish, a theory was put forward that the Irish origin of these words was consciously suppressed by bigoted elites. This text has since been discredited; so much so, in fact, that any claim to an Irish origin for an English word now seems to be suspect.

I believe the following factors might contribute to the depth of feeling in this discussion:

1. In British slang or older English words, the possibility of a Scots-Gaelic origin (rather than an Irish one) can never be completely ruled out.

2. Like most big languages, English is a coalition of regional dialects, and it's worth noting what part of English the Gaelic word entered. In places where Irish and Scottish communities co-exist, we may have to resign ourselves to a certain amount of ambiguity. **Ganzee** (a pullover or undershirt in Jamaica) certainly comes from a Gaelic language,

most probably Irish (**geansaí**), but a Scottish origin can't be ruled out.

3. In American slang, asserting an Irish origin for a slang word (**deas** for jazz music, **sheamus** for a cop) can be in conflict with another minority community (in these examples, African-American and Yiddish).

These are the more controversial ones, as they put the Irish brand – generally, an outgoing and non-confrontational mix of partying and literature – in conflict with communities we have no quarrel with. Sheamus seems to be a happy coincidence; the Yiddish word for a rabbi's assistant, **shamash** (a position notorious for attracting tattle-tales) sounds a lot like the Irish first name, and we all know that lots of Irishmen became policemen in New York. Arguably the fact that both meanings are perceived to be true led to this word being more widely used – is it necessary to insist that it only has an Irish origin? Can't we share? Similarly, the wider implication of saying that jazz comes from *deas* is to say that Irish people have some claim to the origins of jazz, a wild claim that needs more than a coincidence of sounds to support it.

1. *The motive for identifying Irish origins* to English words could be sentimental rather than scholarly. I don't think that etymologists and linguists are spoilsports or bigots for expecting empirical proof for the origin of a word and I'm very happy that attempts to use the Irish language to gloss over the contributions of other cultures in the US are duly challenged. Jazz does not come from **deas**, and

that's okay. This scrutiny isn't limited to words of alleged Irish origin; almost every fun word origin story you've ever heard (Arizona being derived from 'Arid Zone A' or kangaroo meaning 'I don't know' in the Aborigine dialect from a part of Australia that didn't have any) gets exasperated sighs from the linguistics faculty.

2. *The standards of proof typically required.* Grant Barrett, an American etymologist, suggests that in order to prove that a word (say, cowabunga) comes from a particular language (let's say Hawaiian), you need to demonstrate examples of overlapping usage in both languages:

   · Letters, diaries or other writing in Hawaiian using cowabunga in a context equivalent to its use in English;
   · Letters, diaries or other writing in English from people of Hawaiian heritage saying 'as my grandmother used to say, cowabunga!' or a similar display of transference;
   · Examples of English speakers first explaining the word to people they expect to be unfamiliar with it 'Chad is just back from surfing in Hawaii, and he shouts "cowabunga" every time he hits a wave'; and
   · A reasonable demonstration that it couldn't have come from another source (a perversion of Maori *bungee* with Aussie/Kiwi exclamation *cooee* stuck in front for some reason that made sense at the time?).

Words and phrases like *bellissimo*, fajita, *no problemo* and sushi pass these tests easily. Similarly, a term like the Derry slang word 'mucker' to refer to a friend or express empathy with another clearly comes from the Irish for my friend, **mo chara** – this exists as an independent expression with the same meaning and hits all the targets mentioned above. However, **dorc** can mean a single buttock... or someone who is a bit lumpish. Resist the urge to assume that this is the origin of the American English word 'dork', even though that word has unknown origins. Similarly, the Irish word **bogás** means smugness (or self-satisfaction) and has nothing to do with the English word bogus. **Bogásach** means smug.

Barrett emphasizes that a word in English sounding similar to a word in Irish (or any other language under consideration) simply isn't good enough, even if the meanings are alike. The English word may be a dead body, the Irish word may be a weapon, but if you can't place the Irish language at the scene of the crime with a motive, you don't have a case. For the purposes of professional etymologists, a word is innocent of being Irish until proven guilty.

There are a number of practical problems with attributing an Irish origin to an English word with the level of authority expected by an academic, which may overlook a community which was illiterate but outgoing and highly mobile (intentionally or otherwise). This can be particularly frustrating to someone trying to prove lost origins, especially when the default conclusion (that the word is a jabberwock, just made up on the spot) doesn't require such scrutiny.

—⊢Ⅲ-Ⅲ-Ⅱ-Ⅲ-⊢Ⅲ— **Goody Two-Shoes** —⊢Ⅲ-Ⅲ-Ⅱ-Ⅲ-⊢Ⅲ—

One of the Irish words that has certainly burrowed its way into English is a word often used to describe our accent: brogue. And yet, in Irish **brogue** means shoe. So how did this happen? Different English dictionaries all attribute Gaelic as the source (allowing themselves wriggle room for Scots vs Irish) but come up with different explanations as to how it arrived.

Merriam-Webster suggests that it comes from **barróg**, a tight hold. *The American Heritage Dictionary of the English Language* explains that farmers wore brogues and that it must be a reference to this.

None, however, have come up with a chain of evidence such as Barrett has suggested. Sometimes words get appropriated into a new language incorrectly. This, in fairness, proves his point that a similar sound between two words isn't enough to prove a link.

us

Who are we, really?

In the '80s, Morrissey* remarked that the Smiths were more Irish (or certainly no less Irish) than U2, based on the following logic: of the four members of the Smiths, seven of all eight parents were Irish, whereas only three of all eight of U2's parents were from Ireland. I always remembered that remark, as it struck a chord with me: can one person really be more Irish than another Irish person? Is Irishness really defined by whether you are born within specific latitudes or longitudes?

I like to believe there are bonds connecting us greater than geographical happenstance, but I accept that it's hard to pin down what this is in a pithy way that includes our diaspora and our naturalized neighbours. I suspect that the Irish language may hold some clues as to the trough of kinship that connects the grandchild of Irish

* The divisive singer of acclaimed Manchester band the Smiths, not the famed RTÉ sports broadcaster.

emigrants in Boston with the child of Polish migrants in Cork and all the variations in between.

Ní fhágfaidh tú seo go n-óla tú cupán tae – 'you won't leave here until you drink a cup of tea'. The tradition of insisting that you give a guest a cup of tea (and the weird parallel tradition of their refusing it) dates back to the nineteenth century, when a visitor might have no guarantee of food upon their return to their own home – similarly, while in many circumstances it was more expedient to share food than to store it, the risk of taking someone's last morsel frequently shamed guests into not accepting this hospitality. Interestingly, **scál** can mean hot tea or a hero.

Flighty, the classic Irish Mam put-down,* is **aidhmeannach**. Another term for flighty in Irish is **gan fód** – literally, without sod. Figuratively, it means lacking depth or groundedness. **Meabhraigh** means to remind in Irish... not to be confused with **meabhlaigh**, which means to shame. Speaking of Irish Mams, **cnáiscín**, meaning a wooden spoon, may be used figuratively to refer to a disciplinary threat.

---

* Flightiness is a euphemism that covers a spectrum of non-sensible behaviours ranging from poor timekeeping to drug abuse. Such qualities are anathema to the cultural trope that is the Irish Mammy, who is characterized by her hospitality to visitors and cautious nature. The self-sacrificing Irish Mammy is rooted in the Irish literary tradition (Synge's *Riders to the Sea*, Christy Brown's *My Left Foot*, Pearse's poem *The Mother*), primarily by writers who are not mothers themselves.

A spoon is **spúnóg**. If this really means little spoon (with the diminutive suffix -**óg** at the end), is a tablespoon (**spúnóg mór**) a little big spoon?

A **ragaire** is someone who enjoys wandering by night. An **airneánach**, by contrast, is one who enjoys night-visiting – this is a noun and an adjective, in case you were wondering! It comes from **airneán**, a social custom where people would pop by and visit their neighbours for chats and storytelling (rather than anything untoward). Such events may have led to matchmaking. In the Ó Dónaill dictionary, **stócach** means boyfriend, but *Dinneen*'s definition ('a go-between or negotiator who accompanies a man looking for a wife at Shrovetide') makes it seem more like a wingman.

Fadscéalach (literally, long-storied) means loquacious. More extreme than loquacious, a person who is inclined to swear a lot could be described as **mionnach** (a swearword or a curse is **mionn mór**, a big oath). It might be best to keep them away from this next category of person – as well as meaning easily offended, the Irish word **uaibhreach** can mean proud, arrogant and/or lonely. This is different from **iarmhaireacht**, which is specifically the loneliness felt at cockcrow.

Here's a perfectly predictable misunderstanding for this country: the Irish word for unseasonable weather is **anaimsir**, not to be confused with **an aimsir**, which just means the weather. Sunny is **grianmhar** – not to be confused with **greannmhar**, which means funny in a 'ha ha' way. Frost is **siocán**, not to be confused with the word for peace **síocháin**. **Díreog** means a jig – not to be confused with

díreoigh, which means to defreeze/defrost. **Brothall** means heat or sultriness – not to be confused with the English word brothel.

The Irish for the hollow at the back of your knee is **ioscaid**; **tá ioscaid gaoil agam leat** means 'I am [distantly] related to you'. **Is í a máthair bos cos í** means 'she's the image of her mother' (literally, 'she's her mother, palm to foot').

A dó is a dó means two and two, but **tá siad a dó is a dó** means 'they're first cousins'; literally, they're two and two. This explains why the Irish for cousin is **col ceathair** (fourth relation, or fourth prohibition) – **col** means incest or cause for prohibition to marriage and **ceathair** means four, the degree of severity. So, your mother's brother's daughter is on the fourth point (you're point one, mother is point two, uncle is point three and cousin is point four). **Tá siad a dó is a trí** means 'they're first cousins once removed'. First cousin once removed is **col cúigir** (fifth relation, or fifth prohibition).

Many people find the Irish system of cousin counting easier than the English one. Degrees of prohibition were a practical problem in parts of Ireland after the Famine when there literally weren't enough single people unrelated to each other for marriage; *The Playboy of the Western World* opens with Shawn Keogh telling Pegeen Mike, his cousin, of his plans to get a letter of dispensation from the bishop so he can marry her.

The Irish for smoked salmon is **bradán deataithe**. **Deatach** means smoke and, by extension, can be a synecdoche for

a household or hearth. Sometimes smoke and fog mingle;
a love child might sometimes be referred to as a **páiste ceo**
(literally, a fog child). The Irish for fog is **ceo**, tantalizingly
close to the word for music, **ceol**, bringing to mind all sorts
of whispery Celtic mysticism.

The Irish for a spell of nice weather between two showers
is **aiteall**. An unbearable, grating sound (such as fingernails
on a blackboard) is **cíochnach**. On the other hand, **seordán**
means a rustling sound, such as is made by leafy branches
in the wind. A light breeze is **aithleá**. An old Irish term for
horse sense or unschooled wisdom is **gaoith-ghlic**, which
translates literally as wind-wise.

If the idea of wisdom being carried by and learned
from the wind makes you think of magic, you're not alone.
More than a few words in Irish hint at an understanding
of the world that includes the fantastic. **Na huaisle** means
posh people,* but may also refer to fairy folk.
Slabhra means a chain... and may also mean
dowry in the right context. **Slabhra sí** (literally,
a fairy chain) means a daisy chain. **Deora Dé**
(God's tears) is one of the more dramatic Irish

    * *Uaisliú* means
gentrification.

names for fuchsia, and one of the names for a foxglove is
méaracáin na mban sí, which means the banshee thimbles.

Extended family relationships, telling stories, contrary
weather, cups of tea and Celtic mysticism – these are
things we often refer to when we talk about ourselves
and Irishness. However, we have a relationship with the
world and I'd like to look at the things that resonate with
us deeply about who we are and how they connect us to
other places.

ⲖⲖⲖⲖⲖⲖⲖ **Not English** ⲖⲖⲖⲖⲖⲖⲖ

A friend's aunt (a Mayo woman, not that it matters) told me once about a time when she was working as a nurse in a hospital in Manchester with a doctor from Pakistan, who she had great regard for – so much so that she told him that 'even though he was a Muslim, he was one of the most Christian men she'd ever met'. She was extremely surprised that he didn't take it as a compliment, and his tensely polite response hurt more than the honest anger of friends. It took her years to come around to the idea that if she respected him enough to pay him a compliment, it wasn't too much to ask that she express those feelings in a sensitive way.

One of the things you may have noticed about Irish people is that we're not English. Nothing wrong with being English, of course; it's a grand country altogether. Hungary is also a very grand country that isn't Ireland. However, Hungarians tend not to have to explain that they aren't English, why they aren't English or 'kind of' like English people, or why loving their own culture and language isn't a pointed rebuke to the finest aspects of English culture.

Sometimes, when an Irish person accomplishes something in sport or culture, the British media describe them as British.* Ireland isn't unique

* This error mostly occurs in light entertainment and show business journalism. It is not the most serious problem in the world; in fact, it falls into that special category of 'annoyances that are more irritating because complaining about them would make you look petty', even though you are factually correct. The world desperately needs a word for problems of this nature.

in this regard; Scots regularly complain about being British when they win and Scottish when they lose. This process never occurs with Dutch and French celebrities, even those who have lived in the United Kingdom for over a decade, and it's not unreasonable to conclude that the English language might have something to do with it. Countries (or communities) have certain key signifiers – a national language, car, airline, soccer team, brand-name product, rock band, foodstuff – and if they don't have enough of them, they get confused with the nearest big country. Hence Austrians get mistaken for Germans, Lithuanians get mixed up with Russians and Kiwis are tired of showing you how the pattern of stars on their flag is slightly different than that on the Australian one. And so it is with Ireland and the weird concept of Britishness.†

The English and Irish languages have a peculiar relationship here, with Irish borrowing modern words from English out of necessity and Hiberno-English inevitably resting into the creases of Irish. Languages are tailored over time to fit the specific needs and priorities of a particular community, which can be entirely different to those of their neighbours. This often means that, when translated, they can appear overly literal or peculiar to the ear of the receiving language. For example, ripples on water's surface may be called **roic i gcraiceann uisce** – literally, wrinkles on the water's skin (in spite of being the name of a skincare product, **roc** is one of the Irish words for a wrinkle).

† I really wish there was a historically sensitive catch-all expression for people from Britain and Ireland along the lines of Scandinavian or Caribbean, but British will never be it.

Here are some more examples:

A double meaning in Irish is a **leath-thagairt** (literally, a half reference). On an unrelated note, one of the Irish names for the uvula is **sine siain**, literally whining (or whistling) nipple.

Siúcra rua (brown sugar), literally, redhead sugar. I've been told that this may also refer to an attractive redhead.

Seanbhlas means contempt or disgust; it translates literally as old taste (**iarbhlas** means aftertaste).

The Irish for obsession, **aonsmaoineamh**, literally means one thought (or one mind).

The Irish for a baker is **fuinteoir**. A rolling pin is **crann fuinte**, which translates literally as kneading tree. While we're in the kitchen, a phrase for being utterly bored is **dubh dóite**, which translates literally as burnt black.

A wishbone is **cnáimhín súgartha** – literally, play-bone. A playroom is **seomra súgartha**. A mousetrap is **fiodhchat**; literally, wooden cat.

Ficheall is the Irish for chess, which derives from the old Irish **fidchell** (wood intelligence); there was also another chess-like game in olden days called **brandubh** (black raven). **Marbhsháinnigh** means checkmate. Checkmate, of course, comes from the Persian for dead king. If your chess pieces were made out of ivory, that would be **dead** in Irish.

The Irish word for a copy of a book is **macleabhar**, which translates literally as son of [a] book.

One of the Irish names for a white caterpillar is **lámh fhuar**, which translates literally as cold hand.

Whisky is **uisce beatha**, which literally means water of life – a sip or two could lead to someone becoming **fadscéalach** (literally, long-storied), which means loquacious.

⅄⅄⅄ **Between Boston and Berlin** ⅄⅄⅄

The Irish for an adventure is **eachtra**. The word for adventurer, **eachtraí**, can also mean an exile. An alien is **eachtrannach**.

In the twentieth century, a man became president of the United States who was the descendant of poor immigrants who had left for America following a devastating potato blight in the previous century. That man's name, of course, was Dwight D. Eisenhower.

It's impossible to talk about Irish identity without discussing the Irish-American community and the Famine. Something made the assimilation of John F. Kennedy's ancestors different than that of Eisenhower's, even though they had so much in common:

- They were both leaving unborn nations, rather than fully-formed states;
- They were motivated by a regional crop failure; and
- English was not their first language.

What they didn't have in common is more interesting:

- The Irish immigrants had more in common with each other than other groups travelling in those numbers; they overwhelmingly shared a religion, a language and a motive;
- The Irish immigrants faced similar discrimination based on these things, whereas Germans of different religions and resources had less cause for solidarity;

- The Irish clustered in certain cities, where they formed a critical mass;
- The emigrant Irish entirely surpassed their peers back home, whereas Germany had a new native meritocracy; and
- The emigrant Irish were involved in political developments back home, whereas German emigrants weren't (not to the extent to capture Bismarck's attention, at least).

Kurt Vonnegut, one of many German-Americans who fought in the Second World War, lamented the fact that German-Americans felt that they weren't as free to celebrate their own heritage as other communities in the States. He pointed to the First World War as the origin of this problem, noting that the war didn't make a dent in the Italian-American reputation (that came from the mafia rather than Mussolini).

After the Second World War, Germany briefly (on a long enough timeline, forty-five years is brief) shared a key feature with Ireland in that it was partitioned. A critical difference between East/West Germany and Northern/Republic of Ireland was that in Germany the partition did not follow religious population patterns; presumably this was a factor in West Germany becoming secular, tolerant and diverse while the Republic and the North became less so. Culturally, the sense of repulsion towards the recent past made West Germans extremely receptive to new ideas, especially musical trends (from the early work of the Beatles in Hamburg through to techno and industrial, as well as those synth guitars) and to the musical traditions of 'innocent' countries – world music and traditional Irish music.

One German who held Ireland close to his heart was the philosopher Ludwig Wittgenstein, who lived here for a period. Wittgenstein famously remarked that the limits of language were the limits of his world; words shaped thought. This is a popular opinion in Germany, where an infinite number of compound nouns are available to the speaker and the placement of verbs at the end of the sentence protects speakers from interruption (as opposed to the Greeks, for example, who are more likely to frontload the verbs in their sentences). The most famous example of linguistic limitations affecting thought is one made popular by Kurt Vonnegut – the fact that the Romans struggled with algebra on account of numbers also being used as letters. X is always ten.

If words do indeed shape thought, maybe we share some thoughts with another country that uses a similar pair of languages.

⅄⅄⅄ Scotland, Ireland and the ⅄⅄⅄ Sunniest Part of Scandinavia

In 2005, I was at a conference in Scotland where the keynote speaker was Magnus Magnusson. The chair gave him a very thorough and glowing introduction; Magnusson had arrived in Scotland as a child refugee in the Second World War (Iceland was still a dominion of Denmark, which had fallen to the Nazis) and had fought for refugee rights throughout his adult life. He had an excellent academic career in Oxford, earning many distinctions, and had a prolific output as a writer and translator (he translated more Icelandic writing into English than anyone before him, as well as old Norse sagas). Then there was his journalism and charity work. It was a shame, the chair said, that he was best known for being the presenter of a game show when he had accomplished so much more.

When he took the microphone, Magnusson gently reproached the chair, saying that he had no problem at all being associated with *Mastermind*, as it was a show about the best of ordinary people – the passion that drives lay-people to cultivate a love and deep understanding of a subject, and the thirst for knowledge that is more wide-spread than the naysayers would have us believe.

He finished his speech by lamenting how the classical languages had slid out of the general educational curriculum, saying that the slow-earned rewards of these treasures were once available to anyone who was curious to find out more, but were now spoiled by becoming a marker of social class. The old joke 'a gentleman need not speak Latin, but he should at least have forgotten it' told a deeper truth. Posh kids still got to study Latin and Greek, but, like the obscure catechism of good manners, it was now a way for the expensively educated to recognize each other rather than an indicator that someone was privy to the recurring facts and universal truths of Roman history.

This gracious *coup-de-grace* really struck a chord with me. Nine years later, I was reminded of this Icelandic-Cale-donian man of letters during the Scottish Independence Referendum. One of the proponents of the Yes side, when defending their position, came up with a beautifully pithy line: 'The No side think Scotland is the coldest part of Brit-ain, the Yes side see it as the sunniest part of Scandinavia.'

A **mugadán** is a pretentious youngster, or a boy pre-tending to be a man. The utter terror of being seen as 'having notions' or being 'a bit up yourself' is common in postcolonial societies. It's often attributed to a bad attitude

to exploitative authority. This is one of the cultural keystones we share with Scotland.

If there's any country in the world that Ireland shares a simple kinship with, surely it's Scotland? Our Caledonian cousins share a Celtic heritage with us since we were both spared invasion by the Romans. The similarities are so close, in fact, that we can be confused for each other abroad. One such misunderstanding is the insistence by our international friends in calling Irish 'Gaelic'. Because Scotland has more than one native tongue, they need to differentiate between Scots ('*the fleeos wir aachan aboot his heid lik a jobbie'**) and Scots-Gaelic, a language with many similarities in print to Irish.† The first difference you'll see is that the *fadas* point in the other direction.

* This translates as 'the flies swarmed around his head like a shite'.

† They sound quite different.

However, there are some *faux amis* where an Irish word doesn't match its sound-alike in *Gaeilge na hAlban*. Here's a sample of a few:

	Irish		Scots-Gaelic
Tuirseach	tired	**Tùirseach**	sad
Cuan	a haven; to harbour	**Cuan**	the sea
Poca	pocket	**Poca**	bag
Tum	soft, easy	**Tum**	to dip
Bodach	tramp	**Bodach**	old man
Sanas	whisper	**Sanas**	suggestion

Balach	exact	**Balach**	boy or lad
		(*baileach*)	

The biggest difference between Irish and Scots-Gaelic, however, is their relationship with public policy; Scots-Gaelic doesn't have the same legal standing in Scotland that Irish has in Ireland.

─────◁▥▷▁▥▷─────

One Irish name for a fjord is **caolsáile**, which translates literally as narrow seawater.* A glacier is **oighearshruth** (literally, ice stream). Mayo is the proud home of Ireland's only fjord. Poetically, Mayo is also at the crucible of a national debate where many feel that Ireland could have taken a Norwegian approach to the ownership of Ireland's oil and gas resources. Protestors at the Corrib gas line in Mayo include people who think these resources should belong to the state, as well as those with environmental and safety concerns. These concerns are profoundly incompatible with each other, and yet they've been able to work together – very Scandinavian. Norway's presence in the Irish national conversation is most commonly used as an example of a country that did things differently than us and is now doing very well (EU membership, women's rights, fisheries and oil, among other things). Another thing we could borrow from Norway is the word (and the idea) **ildsjel**. Literally, this means a fire soul and means a passionate volunteer involved in everything – every sports club, charity, protest, fundraiser, school board and festival. Norway has made an indirect contribution to the Irish

* A less wonderful name for a fjord in Irish is *fiord*, which just doesn't have the same magic.

language in two ways, one of which was the inspiration that Henrik Ibsen gave to writers of the Gaelic League; the idea that a writer from a small country writing in his own language could cast such a long shadow in the setting colonial sun made him a role model to Pearse and his peers.†
Secondly, it was Norwegian linguist Carl Marstrander's‡ work that brought Irish memoirs like *An t-Oileanach* and *Fiche Blían ag Fás* to an international academic audience; as general editor of the *Dictionary of the Irish Language* and as a widely-published professor of Celtic Studies, he stirred interest in the language and the texts themselves abroad, which encouraged enthusiasts in Ireland (as is too often the case in Ireland, a local creation needs the imprimatur of an international audience before it is deemed worthy of respect at home).

Like Norway, Iceland most commonly turns up in the news in Ireland when it appears to have taken a decisive and morally upright stance on an issue that we are floundering our way towards a cowardly compromise on. In 2009, the joke in the financial markets was that the difference between Ireland and Iceland was 'one letter and six months'. In the months that followed, the different reactions of the two countries to the financial crisis were compared and praised or

† In addition to his status as a champion of small countries and their native languages, Ibsen (in his capacity as a scourge of bourgeois values and 'national pain in the ass') was a key influence on Irish writers in English too, especially Joyce and Sean O'Casey. Synge famously described his works as joyless and pallid.

•

‡ Among his many accomplishments, Marstrander was a champion pole vaulter, which delighted his hosts on his many visits to the West of Ireland.

condemned in accordance with the precast opinions of the commentator in question.

Two place names of interest in Iceland are Írafellsbunga (mountain of the Irish) and Kjaransvík (Ciaran's Bay). These hint at a trading past when Irish slaves,* among other goods, were traded between the islands, as does Vestmannaeyjar, in the Westman Islands – west men is the literal translation of the old Norse name for the Irish. Another such Icelandic place name is Melkorkustaðir, named for an Irish princess turned slave girl called Melkorka, who goes on to become the mother of Ólafr Höskuldsson in the *Landnámabók* saga. Iceland, like Ireland, has a heritage of violent mythology; the Icelandic word *nábrók* (literally, corpse-pants) means the skin of a dead man worn for good fortune.

---

* The existence of Irish slaves in Iceland in the medieval period is a historical fact. The transportation of indentured Irish workers to the Caribbean centuries later was an appalling process that warrants further study, but it was not a slave trade. Saying 'yeah, well, the Irish were slaves too' to a person highlighting the injustices of the slave trade between Africa and the Americas is very bad form – doubly so if it's accompanied by a total lack of curiosity about the details of Irish indentured labour.

Consider these word neighbours from O'Reilly's dictionary:

Danar   Strange, peregrine

In the early 2010s, television audiences in the Anglosphere were suddenly gripped by Dane-mania as *The Killing, The Bridge* and *Borgen* became the boxset binges of choice. The Scandinavian backdrop was unfamiliar and aspirational at the same time, and the crime dramas scratched our whodunit itches in a satisfyingly fresh way. Nobody minded the subtitles at all. A *New Yorker* article at the time offered a theory as to why Danish TV was so good: 'Their largest broadcaster is a cross between NBC and NPR; publicly supported enough to take risks, but with a freedom to sell advertising that keeps them alert to the taste buds of the marketplace.'

I couldn't resist a wry smile when I read this, as it could just as easily have been a description of RTÉ or TG4. But why weren't Irish TV shows selling abroad like Danish ones? It had been fashionable all my life to bemoan the low standard of scripted Irish television, but lately shows like *Love/Hate* and *Pure Mule* have been challenging that assumption. My friend John was working in Copenhagen at the time, and I mentioned this to him.

'It's funny you say that,' he said, 'because when I'm watching a homemade cop show on RTÉ, one of the main things that spoils it is that my suspension of disbelief is completely thrown when the angry police chief is the dad from the Knorr soup ad, and the baddie is played by Bishop

† Irish-Danish relations have improved since O'Reilly's dictionary came out, although a declaration of war against Denmark was still on the statute books until 2014.

Brennan from *Father Ted*.* But when you're actually living in Denmark, it's the same thing with Danish TV – those same actors are in everything. Ads, game shows, radio – you name it.'

'Would you say that these shows actually benefit from that unfamiliarity when they're sold abroad?'

'Well, if the detective in *The Killing* turned up in the ad break telling you to get a flu jab or to come down to the half-price sale at Copenhagen Carpets, would you enjoy it more... or less?'

* The recognition of actors from *Love/Hate* in post-*Love/Hate* RTÉ productions is now a popular drinking game.

The Irish for a Swede is **Sualannach** – not to be confused with **sealánach**, which means a hangman. While it's unlikely that those two words are related etymologically, the word **gotach** – meaning stammering, mumbling or indistinct of speech – does appear to be linked to **Gothach**, a Goth (Scandinavian invader, not a fan of cheerless music). **Co n-iuratar guit báin** – 'fair-headed stammerers [Scandinavians, presumably] will be slain' is a threat/promise offered in *Annals of the Four Masters*.† While once Swedish Vikings bothered the Irish coast, nowadays the main rivalry between our two countries is the likelihood that they will soon break our record for winning the Eurovision more than anyone else. Ireland's pop successes of the late '90s onwards owe more than a little to the backroom efforts of Stockholm production teams – Swedish supremacy in pop music is

† *Annals of the Four Masters* is a chronicle of medieval Irish history.

often attributed to the emphasis on music in their education system.

The Irish words for penny (**pingin**), shilling (**scilling**), market (**margadh**) and slave (**trail**) all came directly from Norse – as the Vikings were bothering the English shores at the same time, some of those words entered English then too. Interestingly, the Norse word for beer, **øl**, is the same as the Irish word for drink.

The Scandinavian countries have been the envy of Irish speakers for decades; they found economic prosperity and didn't have to sacrifice their languages to get it. There would have been more Irish speakers than Swedish speakers at the beginning of the nineteenth century, and both countries experienced serious emigration, but this didn't undermine the language itself; in fact, Swedish exports (especially those from IKEA) make a very big deal of using Swedish words for individual products.

Maybe one of the reasons for this was that these countries were embracing ideas of modernity and liberalism while Ireland was drifting away from them; attacks on Irish have often been presented as an attack on smug, conservative power. But this is no longer the case.

LOVE AND POLITICS

A book came out recently called *The Song Machine: Inside The Hit Factory*, which analyzed recent seismic changes in pop music. Its author, Jonathan Seabrook, proposed that these do not represent a decline or collapse per se, but rather that the way in which music is discussed by critics and their readers took its form during a singular blip in the history of music – the age of the LP album – and technological changes (streaming apps like Spotify) were causing the industry to revert to its true form, the era of the song.

I'll be sad to see the age of the album end; it's what I'm used to and I had no complaints. In particular, I'm a big believer in the idea that songs can show a deeper texture of meaning and resonance when they are played in their intended sequence, like they are chapters in a novel as well as songs in their own right. The best examples of this that come to mind are Stevie Wonder's home run of '70s masterpieces: *Innervisions, Talking Book* and *Songs in the Key of Life*. There was something about the way he'd follow an angry political song ('Living for the City') with a tender love song ('Golden Lady') that made them both more powerful; political events affect people who fall in love and our lives are shaped by the large and small victories and injustices that come our way.

I started @theirishfor in 2015, and before long the Marriage Equality Referendum* was upon us all. It was not so much that love and politics were thrown together as that a light was shone on the places where they already touched and collided.

Ireland has had/enjoyed/endured (delete as appropriate) a reputation as a socially conservative country, especially in matters of sexual health and freedom. Some of this notoriety has reflected onto the Irish language, given that key figures in the beginning of the Republic were also intimately involved in the Irish-language movement; in the acknowledgements of Tomás de Bhaldraithe's† 1959 dictionary, a special mention is reserved in the last

---

* *Pósadh comhghnéis* is Irish for same-sex marriage.

•

† Tomás de Bhaldraithe (1916–1996) was Professor of Irish at UCD and the lexicographer responsible for the first English-Irish dictionary to use the modern spelling and typography. He had begun postgraduate studies in École des Hautes Études at the Sorbonne when the outbreak of the Second World War caused him to leave Paris. In addition to his many academic and administrative accomplishments (getting grassroot and bureaucratic agreement to these changes was no joke), he once built his wife a holiday home as a surprise.

paragraph to say 'the editor is deeply indebted to the Tao-iseach, Éamon de Valera, whose interest in the work has been a constant source of encouragement'.

As someone who is old enough to remember embarrassingly recent milestones like homosexuality being decriminalized and condoms being made available over the counter without prescription, May 2015 was the feel-good moment that the country had been waiting for... and one of its most enduring symbols was a little badge that said 'TÁ'.‡

Here are some words for the things we continue to believe in, even when they make us sad.

---

‡ Don't get me started on the pedants who said that, technically, Irish doesn't have a word for yes and that really *tá* means 'it is'. Technically this is true; *technically* a banana is a herb, and avocados are berries.

The Irish for love is **grá**, not to be confused with **gá**, which means need.

The Irish for cream is **uachtar** and the Irish for president is **uachtarán**. Some literal-minded folk will tell you that this is all to do with cream and presidents being on top, but I can't help but wonder if there's a more profound connection between dairy products and leadership in Irish. After all, milk is **bainne** and a manager is a **bainisteoir**... either way, the opposite of an **uachtarán** would be an **íochtarán** – a pleb, underdog or subordinate. Love can make us feel like either.

Claon means perverse or slanted... not to be confused with **clann**, which means family.

Although the prefix -**il** means many and **stór** means darling, **ilstórach** means a skyscraper – *not* a scoundrel with many darlings.

‹‹‹△△△›››

Smacht means control or discipline; **ansmacht** means tyranny.

The Irish for democracy is **daonlathas**, which comes from **daon**, human and **flaitheas**, rule/sovereignty. **Na Flaithis** also means heaven. **Taoiseach** (an old word for chieftain or lord) is the title of the prime minister of Ireland; the PM of another state is the **príomh-aire**. One of the interesting old Irish names for Satan is **Taoiseach an Bháis** – Prince of Death (there weren't any prime ministers back then).

Whether or not modern **taoisigh** have reached that level of villainy is a matter for posterity, but clearly it is a role that requires a particular set of skills. **Beartaíocht** means cunning, or a high capacity for applied slyness. It's slightly different from **glic**, which more precisely means cop-on/self-preservation rather than calculated manipulation. Such a person might be inclined to use a **sméideog**; this can mean either a nod or a wink (which is handy if you're a blind horse). **Déthoiseach**, meaning two-dimensional, is not to be confused with **Dé** (God) or **taoiseach** (meaning taoiseach).

The Irish language equivalent of nada/zilch/nothing/diddly-squat is **faic** (pronounced 'fwack').* An individual (especially a politician) might be described as cute in Ireland as a reference to their shrewdness rather

* *Dada* can also be used to mean nada/nowt/feck-all/nothing of consequence.

than their appearance. Given that this word doesn't have this meaning anywhere else, it's plausible to think that could be linked to **ciúta**, a gag or a quick remark. One such piece of Mephistophelean political advice which has gone down in history is **ná habair faic agus ná scríobh faic, mar nuair a cuireann tú an dubh ar an gheal tá tú fuckalta, a bhuachaill** – 'Don't say anything, and don't write anything, because when you put the black on the white [i.e. put anything in writing], you are fucked, boy.'†

Although **fear te** translates literally as hot man, it means an unambitious, selfish and/or useless man (who may or may not be hot) in Irish. Similarly, an **áilleánach** is someone who scrubs up well but isn't actually good at anything useful. A more competent individual (or at least one who is not specifically incompetent) is a **slatfhear**, a man who is in good shape (and smartly turned out). It translates literally as wand man.

† Tommy 'the Kaiser' Fitzgerald, *Tig Paud a Chaoin*, Ventry, Co. Kerry.

The wonderfully onomatopoeic **núscar náscar** means someone who is weak and hesitant, who makes bad decisions after lengthy deliberations. Clearly this won't do.

The noun **athaithne** doesn't have an exact match in English; it means the renewal of an old acquaintance-ship. How might such an encounter unfold? The Irish for memory is **cuimhne** – not to be confused with **caime**, which means fraudulence or dishonesty. Similarly, an old friend is **seanchara**, not to be confused with **seachanta**, which means a persona non grata. So maybe the renewal of an acquaintanceship could be disappointing. But maybe not... everyone knows **póg** as the Irish for kiss, but **smais-eog** or **spailp** will also do nicely. A hug is **barróg**, which also means a crested wave. Nuzzling would be **sróinínteacht**. Be careful, however, that all that doesn't lead to **glacaireacht thruaillí** – immodest touching.

The Irish for sex is **gnéas**.* Contrary to the popular myth, there's no connection between the town Naas and the word *gnéas*. Another town prone to saucy misunder-standings is Ballina (**Béal an Átha**), not to be confused with **bealadh**, the Irish word for lubricant. Some people consider that **gnéas** more precisely means gender rather than sex itself, and suggest **ag bualadh craiceann** as an acceptable Irish term for sexual intercourse. However, not everyone is comfortable with its literal translation, whack-ing skin. Whatever you're into. **Caidhreamh collaí** is another term for sexual intercourse; **caidhreamh poiblí**, on the other hand, means public relations.

* Not to be confused with *gréas*, which means needlework.

The Irish word for penis, **bod**, can also mean a tramp or a rude man. A kestrel is **bod gaoithe** – literally, wind tramp... or wind penis (another lovely name for a kestrel is **pocaire gaoithe**, the wind frolicker). **Crann** generally means tree, but can also mean branch, stick, pole or handle. **Crann clis**, literally jump[ing] stick, means penis. Another Irish word for the penis is **toil-fhéith** – literally, lust muscle. Yet another favourite term for the wedding tackle is **falcaire an tinteáin** – the fire-place potato. **Níl aon falcaire an tinteán mar do fhalcaire an thinteán féin**...

Gabháil is one of a number of Irish words for yeast – not to be confused with **gabhal**, which means crotch or junc-tion/gap/road fork – this is the most likely origin of the charming Cork expression **gowl**. The Irish word for vagina, **faighin**, can also mean sheath or case. **Faighin mheala** is a honeycomb – literally, honey case (not honey vagina). **Ábalta** means capable or competent... not to be confused with **bálta**, which is one of the Irish words for vulva.

The Irish for a horn is **adharc**. (Yes, this also can mean an erection.) To blow the horn in Irish is **an adharc a shéideadh**. Officially, the Irish for oral sex is **gnéas béil**, but I've also heard the expression **ag caitheamh boid** (smoking a willy) used in some circles. In the same lewd company, I've heard **teanga dána** for the female equivalent – the bold tongue (this could also be interpreted as the bold language). A sex position is **deasú gnéis** (literally, sex arrangement/ adjustment).

De Bhaldraithe's 1959 dictionary has no word for fore-play.† However, it does have an entry for threesome: **cluiche triarach**.

The Irish for husband is **fear céile** – as opposed to **fear céilí**, a man whose heart belongs only to the dance floor.

---

† What's even more troubling is that foclóir.ie gives *súgradh* as the Irish for foreplay. That can only lead to terrible misunderstandings.

The Irish for gun control is **rialú gunnaí** – not to be con-fused with **rialú gúnaí**, which is dress control. To bear arms or to bare arms... Speaking of the right to bear arms (and prominent advocates of that view), lots of people know **mo chuisle** from *Million Dollar Baby*, a boxing film from the mid '00s in which Clint Eastwood was trying to teach himself Irish. The Irish for flute, **cuisle**, is also the word for a vein. My pulse is **mo chuisle**, which also means my beloved.* My vein, my flute... yep, it's ripe for misunderstandings!

Tóir is a lost eighteenth-century gem from Bishop O'Brien's dictionary which can mean a pursuit (the meaning that is still given in modern dictionaries), but also a burial ground or church property. Such poetic potential here, especially when you consider that the word Tory comes from **tóraí** (an outlaw or robber).† Interestingly, a monster, such as a troll, is **torathar**. Pursuit is the meaning that applies in **Tóraíocht Dhiarmada agus Ghráinne**, one of a number of Irish texts that deal with a woman fleeing from an older fiancé who happens to be a king – *Deirdre of the Sorrows* also covers this subject matter. Interestingly, both Gráinne (who espies Diarmuid at a wedding feast and spikes everyone else's drink so that she can run off with him) and Deirdre (who sees a dead fawn in the snow and declares that her true love will have hair as dark as its fur, lips as red as its split blood and skin as white as the snow) are the instigators of the love affairs that drive these stories; they are not damsels in distress without agency. Having said that, neither story ends well.

* It means my beloved or my darling in the context of it being an abbreviation of *mo chuisle mo chroí*, pulse of my heart.

† There's a Tory Island off the coast of Donegal, but this has a different etymological root – *thúr rí*, the king's tower.

The Irish for a patriot is **tírghráthóir**, not to be confused with **tagarthóir**, an avenger. **Tírghrá**, patriotism or love of country, has been blamed for a lot of the world's problems. Sometimes a country has its moments, though. A general election is **olltoghchán**, which translates literally as great/large election. A referendum, on the other hand, is **reifreann** – not to be confused with **ifreann**, which means hell. The acronym LGBT is LADT in Irish: **leispiacha, aeracha, déghnéasacha, trasinscneacha**.

The Irish for engaged is **dálta**. **Tá siad dálta le chéile** means 'they are engaged to be married'. Another word for engaged is **geallta** – **geall** can also mean a pledge or a bet (marriage is always a gamble, to be fair). The Marriage Equality Referendum was a welcome opportunity for some *tírghrá* after years of national low self-esteem following the collapse of the economy. The scenes in Dublin that day were more like a major sporting victory than an election result. I only wish I had been able to enjoy it. My dad was in hospital the Saturday the results came in and he passed away on the Monday.

Famously, Irish fathers and Irish sons have a fraught and conflicted relationship, a kind of iceberg of disappointments floating in a sea of silence. My experience wasn't like the fathers and sons of John B. Keane plays, but it's still hard to talk about it nearly two years later. Bad memories of school aside, childhood was a happy time for me, and I absolutely hero-worshipped my dad. One of the biggest disappointments of learning to read was that it meant that I now had to do it on my own and not have him read to me anymore. Whenever we'd go for walks in the park or the forest I'd ask him a hundred questions and he'd always know the answer.

The awkwardness of adolescence cut deeply into this bond. However, even during the less congenial points in our relationship, I always saw him as fundamentally unbreakable. Even when he started to have falls, or had to go to hospital for visits that were clearly more than check-ups, it never occurred to me that the time would come when he'd go to hospital and not come back. Irish men are especially useless at talking about the important things, and even fathers and sons who had a great relationship like I did can leave so much unsaid. I never got to thank him properly, or to show him the world he opened my mind to. Every clever or beautiful phrase in a different language reminds me of him.

SEANFHOCAIL

Who doesn't love a good epigram? Nobody, that's who. After all, the simplest definition of poetry is the right words in the right place at the right time. If someone hits a verbal bull's-eye and there are witnesses, there will surely be copycat crimes committed all over town. I've often wondered about the first person to say well-worn lines like 'a stitch in time saves nine' or 'even a broken clock tells the right time twice a day'. I like to imagine someone spitting out their mead (I presume it was a long time ago) and others present high-fiving the smarty-pants who coined the phrase, while someone else present (possibly the butt of the comment being celebrated) tries desperately to think of a better line... and does so, hours after the party is over.*

> * This sensation – thinking of the right thing to say after the moment to say it has passed – is called *l'esprit d'escalier* in French (the spirit of the stairs) or *trippenwitt* (stairs wit) in German.

Such parcels of wit move around quickly. Some people even try to pass them off as their own. I remember my orientation day at UCD when a student union chap had the room in stitches laughing as he reeled off a series of salty rejoinders and sparkling observations describing the perks and pitfalls of campus life to us. A few weeks later, I stumbled upon a copy of *The Irish Male at Home and Abroad* by Joseph O'Connor and noticed that every single line the student union chap had used in his speech had been sourced from this single text. Every single one. I had barely started university and even I already knew you needed to show your work, cite your references and use more than one source.*

Sometimes the parcel of wit becomes too well-known for opportunists to pass off as their own, but something even worse happens – its meaning is misunderstood and the incorrect meaning becomes the accepted interpretation. The classic example of this is 'blood is thicker than water'. Originally, this meant that your fellow soldiers were dearer to you than your physical brothers... because the blood of the battlefield is thicker than the water of the womb. Think about it – if this saying really means what it's generally understood to mean, then what does the water refer to? Also, the fable of the tortoise and the hare was intended to be a warning to hares, not an inspirational tale for tortoises. And don't get me started on 'type A personality' – this was coined by a cardiologist as the highest category of heart attack risk. It was never intended to celebrate certain irritating traits as denoting an entitlement to success.

One of the most extreme recent examples of an epigram

* Later that year, that chap had to resign from his student union role because of his involvement in a sordid scheme to trick freshers into buying past exam papers that were freely available in the library.

detaching from its intended meaning comes from Samuel Beckett. 'Fail again. Fail better' as a quote is far more famous than the text it comes from, *Worstward Ho†*, in which it immediately precedes the narrator lamenting his failing body and contemplating an eternity of illness and vomiting. The inference that repeated failings are stepping stones on the route to success is nowhere to be found in this grim text. However, in defence of those poor souls with 'fail better' tattoos, it's not as if Mr Beckett had, in his long career, written anything more uplifting that they could have chosen instead.

† The only people I know who have read *Worstward Ho* teach literature in universities and have been compelled to do so.

Caveats aside, there's nothing quite like a pre-formed witticism or **seanfhocal** to keep in your verbal arsenal for just the right occasion, and some of these give a lovely insight into a different way of looking at the world. Some are quips, some are turns of phrase, and some are proverbs... maybe not ones you'll see on a matchbox or a sachet of sugar, though.

The Irish equivalent to 'there isn't space to swing a cat' is **níl slí dhá chat chun rince ann** (not the space for two cats to dance).

The intriguing seanfhocal **ní theitheann cú roimh chnámh** means 'a dog doesn't run from a bone'. **Rith madra an dá cháis** (the running of a dog with two lumps of cheese) is an Irish phrase for awkward running. It's been suggested by some that this was transcribed incorrectly by Dinneen and it should be **dá chóis** (two legs) rather than **dá cháis** (two cheeses), but where's the fun in that?

An gruth do Thadhg is an meadhg do na cailíní means 'the son gets attention at the daughters' expense'. Literally, the curds to Thadhg and the whey to the girls (his sisters).

A tense silence in Irish might be called **suan na muice bradaí** – that literally translates as the slumber of the sneaky pig.

Tá an braon nimhe sa cheann aige: 'he has a violent hangover' (a poisonous drop in his head).

Loisc tú do ghual is ní dhearna tú do ghoradh (burnt your coal, didn't get your iron hot) is a way to tell someone they screwed up royally.

Tá craiceann na fírinne air ('it rings true') translates literally as it has the skin of truth on it. Speaking of skin, a great expression for a cruel cheapskate is **d'fheannfadh sé dreancaid ara craiceann** – 'he'd flay a flea for its skin'.

The equivalent phrase in Irish to 'a square peg in a round hole' would be **is é an gabha ag déanamh bróg é** (a blacksmith making a shoe).

An Irish phrase for welcome silence is **amhrán an bhéil dúnta**, which translates literally as the song of a shut mouth. Similarly, **is binn béal ina thost** literally means a sweet mouth is silent.

One of the more colourful phrases in Irish for the sea is **garraí/gairdín an iascaire**, which translates literally as fisherman's garden. Another great phrase/kenning for the sea: **adhbha rón** (abode of seals).

The closest Irish phrase to head over heels, **tóin thar ceann** (arse over head) makes more sense, as your head should be over your heels.

Thit an tóin as an spéir – it was raining heavily (literally, the arse fell out of the sky).

Fómhar beag na ngéanna, literally the little autumn of the geese, is the equivalent expression in Irish to Indian summer. Speaking of geese, here's a great seanfhocal about groupthink or lynch-mob mentality: **nuair a chacann gé, cacann siad go léir** – 'when one goose shits, they all shit'.

Cad é a dhéanfadh mac an chait ach luch a mharú? (What's the son of a cat gonna do but kill mice?) is an Irish spin on 'like father, like son'. Another cat one, **níor loisc seanchat é féin riamh** (an old cat never burned itself) prizes life experience over hereditary qualities. **Chonaic mé cheana thú, mar a dúirt an cat leis an mbainne te** ('I've seen you before, as the cat said to the hot milk') is a spin on the same story; that cat isn't going to burn herself.

Ní troimide an loch an lacha means the lake is not heavier for having the duck on it. This can mean 'the more the merrier' or 'don't sweat the small stuff'. Speaking of anatine matters, the equivalent term to 'acting like a sheep' in Irish is **ar nós na lachan,** which translates literally as... (acting) like a duck.

Lomadh an Luain (literally, Monday shear) is a term for any unlucky or doomed project. Similarly, **margadh an Luain** (a Monday bargain) is an expression for an unlucky deal. This contrasts nicely with:

Aointeach   occurring on (or pertaining to) Friday.

Iontach   wonderful, delightful and/or surprising.

Ag cur madraí i bhfuinneoga is an Irish expression for spoofing or bamboozling someone. It literally means putting dogs in windows. Speaking of dogs and architectural details, **is teann gach madra ar lic a thí féin** (or **ar a thairseach féin**) means every dog is bold on its own doorstep (or threshold).

Ag ithe na feola fuaire (literally, eating the cold meat) is an expression in Irish for talking badly about someone behind their back. If this ever gets back to the individual in question, the following phrase might apply: **méar fhliuch a leagan ar dhuine** (to lay a wet finger on someone) is an expression for challenging someone to a fight.

Tá piobar lena thóin is an Irish expression to describe an excited fellow; it literally means there's pepper in his bum.

Ag iarraidh forais i bhfodhomhain is an Irish expression for attempting an impossible task. It is translated as trying to find the bottom in an abyss.

Nuair a bhíonn an t-ól istigh bíonn an chiall lasmuigh – 'when the drink is in your sense is out'.

Ní ar do ghrideall a bruitheadh é (literally, it was not cooked on your griddle) means none of your business.

On parental love/blindness: **is geal leis an bhfiach dubh a ghearrcach féin** – 'a raven's own chicks are luminous* to her'.

Tá sé ag cur sceana gréasaí – 'it's raining cobblers' knives'.

Is fearr greim de choinín ná dhá ghreim de chat means 'one bite of a rabbit is better than two bites of a cat'.

The seanfhocal **níor chuaigh fial riamh go hIfreann** means 'no generous person ever went to hell' – especially interesting because **fial** has a further meaning: **diabhal**, or devil.

* *Geal* can mean fair-haired, white, bright or luminous, but I think luminous gets the intended humour of the phrase across in this context.

Inis do Mháire i gcógar é, is inseoidh Máire dó phóbal é – 'tell it to Mary in a whisper, and Mary will tell it to the parish'.

Someone who is merely the puppet of a third party might be described as **faoi bhois an chait** – 'under the cat's paw'.

Fan inti means stay in – hold it together at a time of personal crisis.

The Irish for a bathrobe is **fallaing folctha**, tantalizingly close to the English word falling... something you don't want a bathrobe to do. The sadly underused exclamation **dar m'fhallaing!** means 'by my cloak!'

The old-timey simile **chomh géar le súil chailín i lár cuideachtain** means 'sharp as the eye of a gal at a soirée'.

An té is mó a osclaíonn a bhéal is é is lú a osclaíonn a sparán means the person who opens their mouth most opens their wallet least.

Dar fia! is an exclamation of surprise; translations offered in de Bhaldraithe's dictionary include 'Zounds! Crikey! 'Sdeath! Egad! and By Gum!'

A cosy person could be described as **chomh te teolaí le hubh i dtóin circe** – 'as warm as an egg under (in) a hen's bum'.

Another cat phrase – **chomh ríméadach le cat a mbeadh póca air** – means 'as overjoyed as a cat who had a pocket'.

I could literally fill a book with these (others have) but I'm just going to give you a taster for now; these *bon mots* are short and it's only fitting that their chapter should be. It's now time to look at another example of the right words in the right order, something that Ireland has a reputation for being good at.

STORYTELLING
AND MAGIC

The Irish word for an editor is **eagarthóir** – not to be confused with **garthóir**, a screamer.

Every story has a happy ending if you know when to shut up, they say. The art of storytelling is the key to all things. I have never doubted this. As the treasure and debris of our lives touches our hearts and our minds, it curls into story-shaped piles to be stored in our memory. Getting to know someone is getting to hear and understand their story, and falling in love is to be invited to join someone's story and co-write the next part.

But stories have beginnings, middles and ends (not necessarily in that order, of course) and you don't know where you are in your story (or someone else's) until afterwards... assuming we ever know all the pieces. Erin and I first met in 2002 but didn't get married until 2014 after numerous near misses, almosts, misunderstandings and what can only really be described as 'episodes'. So it's not so much a love story as a mosaic of love stories, some funny, some intensely romantic, some with sad endings that would happily turn out not to be endings at all; I think of the way I described first seeing her to my mates in the days afterwards and the way I talk about that memory now when we chat to other parents together.

The way we tell this story now is flavoured by how it all worked out well in the end – details that hitherto had appeared to have no significance are now essential plot points and arguments that were crushing at the time are now hilarious mini-punchlines, retold with grotesquely exaggerated impersonations. The day I asked her to marry me was beset by unforeseen obstacles (if you want to propose to someone in Central Park in autumn, make sure it isn't the same weekend as the New York City Marathon. Also, avoid bottomless Mimosa brunches and tiny dogs, even if they seem friendly from a distance) which, in hindsight, make a better story than if everything ran smoothly.

We remember these moments as being part of a story that we love to tell, but we experience them with our hearts in our mouths, not knowing what'll happen next, and some of the stuff that stories skim over is the very beating heart of life. When you're a couple, everyone asks how you met and fell in love, but nobody asks how you stayed together. The art of storytelling is the key to all things, but it is not all things.

My dad was an outstanding storyteller. In the great tradition of people giving compliments to others that could be as fairly given to themselves,* he once remarked

* The greatest example of this is Tom Waits describing Johnny Cash's singing as 'sounding like the penitent thief who was crucified next to Jesus'. Surely that description applies as much to Mr Waits as it does to Mr Cash.

(while 'The Lakes of Pontchartrain' played on the radio) that Christy Moore was a decent songwriter, but his real craft was to interpret the songs of others better than they ever did themselves. While Dad didn't sing, he retold stories better than he found them and characters from his hometown or his schooldays took on a semi-mythical status from his descriptions. To actually meet some of these chaps in real life was quite disorientating.

I've come to believe that the same truth can be told badly or well without being broken either time. In both journalism and poetry, it all comes down to the right words in the right order.

George Orwell's essay 'Politics and the English Language' advocates a lean, undressed writing style; the last three words of the title are especially significant. **Seoraí** might be the most Irish word in Irish; it means the flourishes and stylish additional details in storytelling, the kind that separate it from a mere recounting of facts and actions. These flourishes are quite different from exposition, the practical information the storyteller is obliged to tell you for the imminent events and character decisions in the story to make sense. The Irish word for exposition, **réamhléiriú**, may also mean rehearsal.

Nobody likes exposition (and not many people like rehearsal either) and genre fiction, for all its purported lack of prestige, can avoid much of this by using certain tropes that are already well-known to its readers. Detective stories are one such genre. The Irish for a detective is **bleachtaire**, which can also mean a milk-dealer. A **scéal bleachtaireachta** is a detective story... as opposed to **scéal beachtaireachta**, which would be a story about beekeeping.

Lucht leanúna (literally, following people) can mean religious devotees, followers or fans. The Irish for fan fiction is **ficsean lucht leanúna**.*

A **seanchaí** is a very special kind of storyteller – an oral historian and a custodian of old traditions. But there are other types of storytellers doing the rounds, and you may want to watch out for them. A **scloitéir** is someone who over-indulges on food and drink. It may also refer to someone without storytelling talent who proceeds regardless. Another word for a talentless storyteller is **strambánaí**, which may also mean a longwinded, boring person.

* Perhaps the Irish for fangirl should be **Lean-Úna**?

The Irish for novel is **úrscéal**, a new story. **Úr** can mean a grave as well as new, so a novel could be considered to be a grave story; this double meaning was not lost on Máirtín Ó Cadhain, the author of *Cré na Cille*, widely regarded as the greatest novel in the Irish language. *Cré na Cille* is set in a graveyard where the deceased characters are doomed to spend eternity dwelling on the petty, local squabbles that bothered them when they were alive. The idea of the Irish language being committed to the grave but refusing to shut up is a deeply resonant one. As a genre, the novel is intimately associated with the rise of the middle class in Europe, as literacy, printing, leisure time and disposable income made the format possible. The historical circumstances of the Irish language and the people who spoke it meant that the novel was not the obvious format for literature *as Gaeilge*, where a tradition of verse and bardic poetry prevailed.

Dámh	the literary caste
Ánradh	bardic poet of the second order
Clí	bardic poet of the third order
Cana	bardic poet of the fourth order

As you can probably deduce from the list above, there's more to becoming a bard than declaring yourself to be one and a range of ornate and intricate poetic metres exist in the tradition. **Comhardadh** is a type of bardic rhyme; **comhardadh briste** requires identity of vowels and agreement of consonants in quality. **Comhardadh slán** has the same restrictions but also requires consonants to agree in class as well as quality.

A temporary period of calm at sea is **deibhil**, which is also the name of an intricate kind of poetic metre in Irish. **Aicill** means a rhyme between the last word in one line of a poem and a word in the middle or start of the next line.

Ballybeg, where so many of Brian Friel's plays were set, comes from **baile beag** (small town) in Irish. Friel's play *Translations*, which was first performed during the politically charged days of the hunger strikes (its cast including a then unknown Ballymena actor called Liam Neeson), was set around a hedge school at the time of the Ordnance Survey of Ireland where place names were deliberately and carelessly anglicized; examples presented include Burnfoot for **Bun na hAbhann** (bottom of the river) and Swinefort for **Lis na Muc** (the fort of the pigs). One of the characters who is horrified by these proceedings observes that 'it is not the literal past, the "facts" of history, that shape us, but the images of the past embodied in language'.

As we have seen, translation is a subtle craft surrounded by pitfalls. A near neighbour and near contemporary of Friel's was Seamus Heaney, who also addressed the ideas of language, identity and history in his work. Heaney found that Hiberno-English contained in its phrasing and rhythms the possibility for translating classical and old English texts in a way that would more closely preserve their flavour and energy. Heaney's *Beowulf* resolved an interminable debate about that poem's opening line – should *hwæt* be a standalone interjection, or does it change the meaning of the rest of the sentence – with the Ulster vernacular 'so'.

The Irish word **eachtra** means a tale of high adventure.

I've alluded to *An Táin** before now, but I'd like to give it special mention here because it's the work that I had the opportunity of studying in primary school, secondary school and university. Not in the same way, of course. In primary school, *An Táin* was read to us as a straight-up adventure tale; Cúchulainn was a hero, the Red Branch Knights were his band of merry men who were cursed by a mean witch to experience childbirth pains, and Queen Medb was a baddie.

In secondary school, however, a different approach was taken. We had a brilliant, outspoken feminist teacher

* The *Táin* is an epic poem (like the *Oddysey*) in the Irish tradition. It concerns the fallout of an argument between a married couple over who is richer, which leads to the theft of a brown bull of Cooley.

who explained to us how *An Táin,* like so much Ulster mythology especially, was all about gender roles – the story is kicked into action by an argument between a married couple, the 'pains of women' that the Red Branch Knights were made to feel were actually menstrual cramps rather than childbirth†, characters with gender ambiguity have great insight or power and much kingly power rests upon the pampering of fragile masculinity. We were open to such ideas as teenagers – it was a little bit dirty and consistent with the Freudian interpretations of fairy tales that we were finding out about.

In university I studied Anglo-Irish literature and was exposed to certain plays by Yeats‡ involving Cúchulainn, Emer and other old favourites. While these plays discuss a lot of profound ideas with great seriousness, they bear absolutely no relationship to the swashbuckling adventure stories we were told in primary school. I think of the three threads of Cúchulainn and I've come around to the point of view that the different interpretations reflect well on the

† The debate as to whether the 'pains of women' felt by the Ulstermen are childbirth or menstrual is ongoing; supporters of the latter theory state that the curse causing the pains also gives the knights a capacity for great rage in battle, making them most fearsome. They also point out that the childbirth theory gained acceptance because it's easier to present to pre-pubescent children.

‡ It's no slur on W .B. Yeats to say that his plays are less accessible to modern audiences than his poetry, especially his early love poems.

richness of the original content; rather than contradicting each other, they show the possibilities of storytelling and how mythology endures by meaning more than one thing at a time.

There's a popular theory that Bram Stoker got the name for Dracula from the Irish **droch fola**, meaning evil blood. This appears to be a retrofitting; unlike some other writers who are cursed by academics to this day, Stoker kept extensive, clear notes on his research and *droch fola* isn't in there. *Droch fola* is excellent wordplay nonetheless, and deserves to be remembered on the condition that it is seen as such.

Misunderstandings involving the old Irish alphabet might explain the (totally incorrect) theory that Tolkien got Sauron's name from Irish. The old Irish word for an emperor or Caesar is **Saesar**, but the lowercase **s** and **r** in Dinneen's dictionary make it appear like **Saeran** to the untrained eye.

The Irish for orc is *orc*.[*] I don't know which came first; it's in Irish dictionaries that predate *The Lord of the Rings*, but that doesn't mean Tolkien got it from Irish. As with Bram Stoker and *droch fola*, the Irish language isn't served by jumping to flimsy conclusions that might associate it with widely-beloved works. We know that Tolkien, who visited Galway as an external examiner in the '50s, didn't care for the Irish language after attempting to study it, declaring it 'a mushy language' that suffered from 'fundamental unreason'.

Tolkien famously declared 'cellar

[*] *Orc* might be linked to *arc* or *arcán*, an intruiging lost word for a piglet. An arcane piglet, if such a wonderful beast exists, would be an *arcán rúnda*.

door' to be the most beautiful combination of syllables to an English-speaker's ear when word meaning was disregarded (the combination of sibilant, labial and soft denotative syllables in that order, if you want to be technical) – hence the poetic impact of words like lore, nevermore, Elsinore. He declared the Welsh language to be beautiful on account of its many cellar doors. Presumably he never heard of *Dún an Óir* in Kerry or he might have extended the compliment to Irish. He did admit that **nazg** (the Black Speech word for the One Ring) was similar to **nasc** (a link in a chain, a bond), a word he was familiar with. He did, however, claim that this similarity was not intentional.

Tolkien was a student of many languages and folklore, and lamented the poverty of a truly English corpus of mythology, a shortfall he attempted to address with his own writings. He was especially interested in the power of allegory and how it could communicate his Christian ideas, an interest he shared with his Northern Irish friend C. S. Lewis. The story goes that they had vastly different experiences in the First World War; the sensitive Tolkien was shaken to the core by the carnage while Lewis earned the nickname 'the Belfast Butcher' from his comrades for his soldierly enthusiasm. Their friendship began while Lewis was still a confirmed atheist, and it was a series of animated conversations with Tolkien that led him back to Christianity.

A common complaint about social media and the modern world in general is that it's easier to avoid contact with people you disagree with and that our sense of the middle ground is lost as our opinions are reinforced by our selective and atypical company. While people sometimes 'hate-read' articles by gadfly columnists they despise in order to fire themselves up, we read journalism in a different way than we read other prose. Maybe we're reluctant to engage with works we expect to disagree with. Perhaps we always have been.

Whenever I'm asked to name a book I have enjoyed but disagreed with, I usually answer *The Screwtape Letters* by C. S. Lewis. I'll never share the author's zero-sum take on Christianity and his bitter dismissal of romantic love. But the writing is outstanding – that such ostensibly cerebral ideas could be presented with such clarity by a narrator with so much snark and swagger is enough to make any writer very jealous. The concept of chronological snobbery (viewing previous generations as less intelligent or caring for their lack of our hindsight, as though the past is a bad neighbourhood) is one of many that I keep returning to. In particular, Lewis's representation of hell as a cliquey bureaucracy full of petty rivalries, backstabbing and monthly targets is as relevant as ever. 'Bring food or be food', the warning Screwtape gives to his young demonic protégé, could be a sinisterly inspirational quote on many an office wall today.

Great writing is never just about one thing, and it's unlikely that I'd have read an unvarnished thesis on Christian morality as quickly or as willingly as I read *Screwtape*. Great writing, in stories and in speeches, matches the right technique to a great idea and leaves no trace of the frustrations and labour that produced it. Certain writers, however, do not get the opportunity to display their arsenal of literary techniques; they are compelled to express the ideas of others in a manner that leaves no room for subplots, metaphors or irony. More precisely, I mean my colleagues in the modern-day Screwtapish government departments, where legislation is laboriously written, re-written, challenged and finally rewritten... until the next election.

Which takes us from the charmed world of language in storytelling to the Dantesque hell of bureaucratic language.

LANGUAGE AND THE BUREAUCRACY

The Irish for tax is **cáin**, not to be confused with **caoin**, which means to keen or lament. In the United States, it's been said that the tax code is 'longer than the Bible but with no good news'. It's not much shorter in Ireland (or anywhere else that I know of, for that matter). Aside from the actual amount you hand over, tax is a long and complicated business wherever you go. In fact, it's a bit like learning a new language.

But why are the testaments of governments so long-winded and confusing? I asked an older colleague about this some years ago, and I always remember his response. 'Every individual law or bit of legislation starts off like the Ten Commandments. Then someone asks if you could clarify what exactly you mean by covet... and who exactly you mean by neighbour... and what is implied by shall... and before long you've enough footnotes and sub-paragraphs to fill an Old Testament.'

Obviously, that view contains the tired wisdom of

someone who's seen bureaucracy from the inside, and not everyone shares it. There are a lot of people who believe that tax is complicated by design, that the financial advice sector would be decimated if the tax acts were shortened and put in plain English. **Líodóireacht** means toadying or sneaky, ingratiating talk; this is in no way connected to **dlíodóireacht**, which means practising law.

Consider the following extract from the Taxes Consolidation Act, 1997:

> In computing the charge to tax in respect of sums received by any person which are chargeable to tax by virtue of this section (including amounts treated as sums received by such person by virtue of section 87), there shall be deducted from the amount, which apart from this subsection would be chargeable to tax any loss, expense or debit (not being a loss, expense or debit arising directly or indirectly from the discontinuance itself) which, if the trade or profession had not been discontinued, would have been deducted in computing for tax purposes the profits or gains of the person by whom the trade or profession was carried on before the discontinuance, or would have been deducted from or set off against those profits or gains as so computed.[*]

Pure poetry, I'm sure you'll agree. While some people relish this kind of writing, I'm fairly certain that the officials who put this together (and the students who are compelled to study it) would have loved to have just said 'you' instead of 'any person which are chargeable to tax' and 'your previous business'

[*] Taxes Consolidation Act 1997, 91 (4) (a).

instead of 'the trade or profession was carried on before
the discontinuance'. However, every graceless phrase in
that paragraph is in there because of a legal precedent, one
where a simpler previous phrasing ended up costing someone a lot of money.

This isn't limited to taxation – examples that involve
the money in someone's own pocket tend to catch the
attention more than something as abstract as pollution,
road safety or prison overcrowding. One example of grammatical minutiae leaning deeply into a piece of civil service
writing is the Anglo-Irish Agreement of 1985, when late
night arguments were held over the placing of a comma.
The offending sentence was 'Britain has no selfish strategic
or economic interest in Northern Ireland' or 'Britain has no
selfish, strategic or economic interest in Northern Ireland'.

Moving, isn't it? Now imagine translating it into Irish.

The current position in the Republic of Ireland is that
Irish is the first language of the state.† This doesn't extend to
treaties with other countries (like the Anglo-Irish Agreement referred to above), including EU treaties, and there
are situations when legal precedents in England may apply
in Ireland. However, it does mean that
citizens are entitled to conduct their
business with state agencies in Irish if
they please, and that the Irish version
of the constitution is the primary text.

† As per Article 25.5.4
of the constitution.

In practice, this last part shouldn't matter if dictionaries
were just exact word-mirrors of each other, but as we've
seen so far, that isn't always the case.

While it was long understood that the constitution was
written in English and then translated into Irish, recent
scholarship supports the opinion that the two versions

were composed simultaneously, with special consideration given to the phrasing used in one version when there was ambiguity in the other. For example, in Article 12.4.1, which addresses the age at which a person may be elected president, any confusion around the English wording 'who has reached his thirty-fifth year' can be settled by checking the Irish wording **gach saoránach ag a bhfuil cúig bliana tríochad slán (is intofa chun oifig an uachtaráin é)**, which more explicitly rules out thirty-four-year-olds.

There are points in the constitution where the same English word is translated differently at different points. For example, recognized is translated as **admhaigh** in several places, but as **glactar leis** in Article 8.2, the section in which English is acknowledged as a second official language. **Glac** would be seen as a less enthusiastic form of acceptance than **admhaigh**; to put this in context, *admhaigh* can also mean to admit openly, even confess in church or to God, whereas *glac* can mean to tolerate or accept, and is used to refer to the handling of horses.

Having said that, you could spend a pleasant month wandering the Four Courts in Dublin without once hearing a lawyer cite the difference between the wording of the same law in English and Irish in a case. It's only ever a final measure used in particularly controversial, hard cases... and you know what they say about hard cases.* When it comes to controversial, hard cases, one topic beats them all.

* 'Hard cases make bad law.'

Abortion † has been a political hot potato in Ireland for decades, and the Eighth Amendment ‡ remains the most famous example of a difference in wording between the Irish and English version of the constitution. Both versions of the text were presented to voters in 1983. § I've presented them both for your consideration:

> *In English:* 3 The State acknowledges the right to life of the <u>unborn</u> and, with due regard to the equal right to life of the mother, guarantees in its laws to respect, and, <u>as far as practicable,</u> by its laws to defend and vindicate that right.

> *As Gaeilge:* 3 Admhaíonn an Stát ceart na <u>mbeo gan breith</u> chun a mbeatha agus, ag féachaint go cuí do chomhcheart na máthar chun a beatha, ráthaíonn sé gan cur isteach lena dhlíthe ar an gceart sin agus

---

† I respect the fact that you bought this book out of an interest in the Irish language and not because of a willingness to receive my personal views on this topic, so I'll refrain from deviating beyond my brief.

•

‡ In Ireland, the Eighth Amendment, which became Article 40.3.3. following a referendum in 1983, is the section of the constitution that covers this area. This is not to be confused with the Eighth Amendment in the United States, which prohibits cruel and unusual punishment.

•

§ All changes to the Irish Constitution, including EU treaties, require a referendum.

ráthaíonn fós an ceart sin a chosaint is a shuíomh lena dhlíthe <u>sa mhéid gur féidir é</u>.

In this instance, the Irish-language version has been phrased more strictly than the English version. 'Practicable' is usually translated as **indéanta**, but **féidir**[*] (which is less ambiguous, translating as 'can') is used in the Irish version. **Beo gan breith** is not a literal translation of unborn, but more specifically means the living who are not born. 'Defend and vindicate' are combined in the word **chosaint**. The politicians proposing the amendment were advocating a very hard line on the issue, and fears that a literal translation may have unintentionally led to a softer position no doubt dictated the word choice in the Irish version. It certainly isn't the case, as has been mooted, that limitations within the Irish language itself have made laws more restrictive or conservative than they would otherwise be.

[*] When Barack Obama visited Ireland, he told adoring crowds *is féidir linn* – yes we can.

The Republic of Ireland isn't unique in having laws in more than one language. Treaties and directives in the European Union have to be workable in the various languages of the member states. As you can imagine, a subtle difference between the Swedish and Italian words for 'workplace' could have expensive legal consequences unless suitable precautions are taken. These directives and treaties have to be incorporated into the local laws of the member states, but it wouldn't go down well if one state chose to weasel out of an agreed unpopular decision on the basis that 'employee' or 'military spending' had a different meaning in their native tongue.

One such precaution is a concept in jurisprudence: the teleological interpretation of a text (as opposed to a systemic one). A teleological interpretation is one that privileges the intended purpose of a law over the nuances of the wording in the event of a disagreement over phrasing; the opposite of this is a systemic interpretation, which is more common in single-language jurisdictions.

The translation of Acts of the *Oireachtas*† into Irish is frequently cited as an example of the Irish language and its proponents being a drain on the public purse. If it continues to be an administrative chore outsourced by different government departments at different timeframes, the only objective met will be the legal obligation. But if it were a strategic and centralized function, it could actually be of great service. In a country where multiple government departments, agencies and local authorities use different working definitions in English of key terms like 'homeless', 'living as man and wife' and 'long-term unemployed' among many others, people can fall through the cracks – a person might be too homeless/married/unemployed for one service and not homeless/married/unemployed enough for another. The scrutiny involved in the translation process could identify these gaps and mismatches where they occur. Also, if the legislation is particularly obtuse in English ('the charge to tax in respect of sums received by any person which are chargeable to tax by virtue of this section', for example), maybe the Irish version could, would and should be clearer – that would be a real service.

† The parliament of the Republic of Ireland.

Sometimes the wrigglings and wranglings of the legislative process would almost make you yearn for a simpler era. The past only seems simple with hindsight, though – for example, the pre-Norman era in Ireland when Brehon Law applied could be just as capricious and intricate as today's health and safety regulations. As early as the seventh century and without a Latin-Roman framework to base it on, Brehon Law (**breithe** means a judge) covered areas such as:*

Family Law: Nine specific forms of sexual union are defined, ranging from **lánamnas comthinchuir**, where both the man and the woman are property owners, to degrees of concubinage (with or without consent of the woman's family) and finally to the union of two insane persons. A woman could seek divorce from her husband on a number of grounds, including: if he became too fat to make love, if he was a miser, if he tricked her into marriage using sorcery or if he composed a satire about her. She may also leave her husband if he chooses another woman, but she may elect to stay: (non-fatal) injuries inflicted by a first wife upon a second wife did not have legal consequences;

* These examples have been taken from *A Guide to Early Irish Law* by Fergus Kelly.

Contract Law: A wife could dissolve unfavourable contracts (**dochor**) that were entered into by her husband;

Copyright Law: In a case that foreshadowed the

Facebook lawsuit centuries later, Colmcille (back when he was still just Columba) borrowed his friend Fintan's illuminated gospel, and proceeded to make his own copy without permission. The outrageousness of this act was compounded by the fact that Colmcille's version was superior to the original. The judgement given, **la cach mboin a boinín** (to every cow her calf), meant that Colmcille was required to surrender his work to Fintan.

Satire: It was a mark of respect to poets and their influence that misuse of their talents was so carefully regulated. **Áer** were satirical acts that could cause the satirist to be fined the victim's honour-price; this included composing a satire that was so on point that it was repeated elsewhere (an early version of 'going viral'). **Moladh donigh aoir** is praise/atonement from a satirist that satisfactorily washes away insult.

Property: Morsels of food craved by a pregnant woman could be taken without punishment.

Murder: A distinction is made between secret murder (**duinetháide**, the theft of a person) and a killing that was acknowledged openly. As the outcome of a murder trial would usually be the payment of compensation (that 'honour-price' again) to the victim's kin, special provision had to be made for kin-slaying (**fingal**). A man found guilty of the murder of a woman would have his hand and foot cut off before he was put to death.

Bees: The trespass of bees onto neighbouring lands and the responsibility of their owner for injuries inflicted on their travels was written about at length in Brehon legal texts, as were rights of ownership to hives found on public land and tributes to be paid in honey.

The journey from Brehon Law judgments about the trespassing of bees to EU directives on the maximum pollen content allowable in a pot of honey is a long one. It's a journey that starts in an era when people lived in small communities and knew everyone and only the very brave made long trips. It moves into a time when people started trading with outsiders who had different laws and different languages, different ways of resolving the same problem. It went through periods of destruction and chaos when no law applied other than brute force, and other periods when conflicting powers co-existed, jostling for legitimacy. It has now arrived in an era when some denounce honey as an unhealthy form of sugar and others praise it as a miracle cure for various ailments, where scientists and lawyers in corporate boardrooms argue over whether they can get away with calling a honeyless product honey-flavoured or not. It's a world where different states can have different rules for these things, and a state with lax rules may sell honey (or whatever else) to a state with strict ones. It's not a land of certainties or short, simple, satisfying answers, and where tidy certainties have to make room for untidy truths.

Sadly, not everybody is happy to sacrifice a little certainty for a little truth. In the same way that an angry fool cannot see past a bee's sting to appreciate their stable society, their patient labours, their care for their young, their ecological contribution and their insistence on only using violence as a last resort, some people cannot see past the sting of a single regulation or directive to the hive of law-bound democratic institutions that deem it necessary. A terrifying development of recent times has been the rise of reactionary traditionalists and nationalists who want to discard the hard-won treasure of peacetime to return to an imaginary past, a Tír na nÓg in their imagination. But nobody ever returns to or from Tír na nÓg.

It's my fervent wish that the Irish language never becomes a part of a Tea Party movement in Ireland. For all the thrills of Cúchulainn's adventures and the delights of Brehon Law, for all the exquisite poetry and wordplay locked into the simplest sentences, treating the Irish language as a perfect place just out of reach does it a disservice. It tells us a lot about the way we were, but it's still telling us about the way we are. All the good old stuff is still there but it's still flexing and picking up new material. I'm looking forward to seeing the first entries in the *foclóir* listed as loanwords from Polish and Igbo. I'm hopeful to see more Irish words enter common use in English. And maybe, just maybe, I'll give my surname to someone over the phone soon and they'll ask 'Is that with a silent ghdh, sir?'

CONCLUSION
Candlelight

Thomas Edison's invention of the light bulb was initially greeted with some scepticism; it appeared to be a solution for a problem that nobody had. Candles, whale oil and other light sources were widely available, and didn't require the infrastructure necessary to make Edison's device work. His reply to these concerns is now famous: 'We will make electricity so cheap that only the rich will burn candles.'

The invention and ascent of the light bulb didn't destroy the candle sector, but it changed the way we see candlelight entirely – sometimes romantic, sometimes spiritual, good to set an atmosphere (maybe even perfumed) and handy to have in an emergency. I can't think of candlelight without smiling a little: I think of my wife and the candle-lit meals we've had, or the power cuts we've weathered together brightened with a single flame, or the candle we lit together on our wedding day. I think of my daughter's name and the beauty of a flame reflected in a glass of red wine. I think of protest marches and vigils held at night, or concerts with ten thousand cigarette lighters in the air.

It's hard to write about Irish with any respect or affection without being dragged into a defence of state policy or an explanation for its continued existence. I've resisted this while running @theirishfor because I think the best defence of Irish is the beauty of the language itself. It means different things to different people, and being free from any group or position has allowed me to present a whole spectrum of its colours, from old Irish in pre-standard fonts to the slang on *Gaelscoil** playgrounds. But it would be churlish of me to avoid the subject altogether before I say goodbye.

The Irish language is not unlike candlelight – beautiful and fragile, romantic and practical, but scary to those who've been burnt before. Candles work the way they've always worked, but now that the world has changed we see them differently and have different expectations. And while old-fashioned, simple candles still exist, new kinds of candles have now also become available. What's more, light bulbs and light fixtures have been developed to replicate the candlelight effect – never the other way around.

* Schools where lessons are taught in the Irish language.

If I could change one thing about the way Irish is taught in school, I'd make Irish more than one subject, the same way that mathematics is more than one subject (a student can exercise their mathematical talents in accountancy and applied maths as well as the general maths course). For example, one curriculum could focus on using Irish in practical interactions with the state: the application forms, planning permissions, the political system and the constitution, practical matters which were never taught to me in school. Another curriculum would centre on Irish literature and mythology, the kind of beautiful writing that some feel represents the whole point of saving the language in the first place. Another could focus on spoken Irish, and so on. Allowing students to pick the Irish syllabus that suited them best (and having the option of picking more than one if they wished) would reduce the resentment that comes with a subject being presented as compulsory, and the advantages attached to doing well in Irish (traditionally seen as a hard subject to do well in) would increase sharply.

For me, rediscovering Irish was all about trying to understand my dad better as I realized that I was about to lose him forever. Every time I find an obscure old word or quirky turn of phrase it reminds me of him; the candlelight flickers for a moment. I go to work, I pick up groceries, I cook the dinner, I try to be a better dad, husband and son. It's easy to get overwhelmed by the list of chores and the endless bills, the worries both real and imagined. I try to remind myself of the reasons that I put up with it all. I come home and open the door to see my wife waiting for me, her smile shining in the candlelight. We tiptoe upstairs and have a peek at Lasairíona as she sleeps.

As I write this, my daughter is eleven months old, her first word an eon away. I speak to her and have no idea if the noises out of my mouth could ever mean as much to her as the perfect, experimental sounds out of hers mean to me.

One day, if I'm as lucky as she makes me feel, she'll want to ask me where the water in the tap comes from, why the people in the telly have gone to sleep and how early she's allowed to get out of bed on Christmas morning. And I'll want to tell her about how **maológ** means the amount over the brim that something has been filled, how **órshnáithe** means a golden thread and how **lómhar** can mean either woolly or precious. The big candle lights the little candle, and the little candle keeps burning.

ACKNOWLEDGEMENTS

I had wanted to write books from the time I was able to read them, but by my mid-thirties I was starting to lose faith that this would ever happen. I am eternally grateful to the following people who helped turn my dream into a reality.

Motherfoclóir is a continuation of the work that started on my @theirishfor twitter account. The goodwill towards that project helped make this book possible, and I am grateful to everyone who has followed, liked, retweeted and supported that account. You are all amazing and wonderful and it's a thrill to know there are so many other wordnerds out there.

My agent Sallyanne Sweeney believed in this project from the very start and fought for it tirelessly while also giving invaluable advice and insights. Thank you for seeing more potential than I did in my first scribblings and for always being at the other end of the phone.

Only writers truly see the invisible magic that great

editors work upon their books, so I can assure you that Neil Belton is truly a brilliant editor. Thank you for saving me from myself. I would also like to thank the rest of the team at Head of Zeus, especially Clémence Jacquinet, Victoria Reed and Suzanne Sangster. I would also like to thank Simon Hess and Declan Heeney at Gill Hess for all their work.

Thank you to Michael Freeman and Emer McLysaght (at the Daily Edge), Ed Smith (at Today FM) and Carl Kinsella (at Joe.ie) for doing features on @theirishfor in its early days and bringing it to the attention of thousands of new followers. Peadar Ó Caomhánaigh, Michelle Ní Eidhin, Derek O'Brien, Doireann Ní Griofa, Rudhán Mac Cormaic and Siún Ní Dhuinn were all kind enough to offer their expertise to me on occasions when my own was lacking.

Lisa McInerney and Amy Rosenbaum gave me timely, brilliant advice when I first stepped from the safe, solitary shore of writing into the choppy waters of the book business. I'll never forget it. I'm also grateful for the friendship, wisdom, support and encouragement I've received from Joe Griffin, Alan Gaffney, Tom Gallagher, Peter Sheehan, Mal McCormack, Paul McMahon, Roger Connolly, Lisa Coen, Sarah-Davis Goff, Sarah Maria Griffin, Alan Maguire and Sinéad Burke.

My Mam put up with a lot while she was dragging me up, and I'll never be able to thank her enough. I hope I can find half as much patience, kindness and common sense in myself as I proceed on the parenting journey. It's great to know that the mistakes I make as a Dad might be alleviated by the presence of an incredible grandmother nearby.

Finally, I want to thank Erin, my wife. I was lucky to fall in love with the best person I've ever met and luckier to be loved back. Thank you for giving me everything I have that matters.

Darach Ó Séaghdha
Dublin, July 2017